FOR YOU,
FOR YOU I AM
TRILLING
THESE SONGS

FOR YOU, FOR YOU I AM TRILLING THESE SONGS

Kathleen Rooney

COUNTERPOINT
BERKELEY

Library of Congress Cataloging-in-Publication Data

Rooney, Kathleen, 1980–
    For you, for you I am trilling these songs / by Kathleen Rooney.
        p. cm.
    ISBN-13: 978-1-58243-545-9
    ISBN-10: 1-58243-545-6
    1. Rooney, Kathleen, 1980- 2. Young women—United States—Biography. 3. Young adults—United States—Biography. 4. Women authors, American—Biography. 5. Feminists—United States—Biography. 6. Young women—United States—Social life and customs—21st century. 7. Young adults—United States—Social life and customs—21st century. 8. United States—Social life and customs—1971- 9. Edgewater (Chicago, Ill.)—Biography. 10. Chicago (Ill.)—Biography. I. Title.

    CT275.R779A3 2010
    977.3'11044092—dc22

                                    2009038081

Cover design by Ann Weinstock
Interior design by Megan Jones Design

Printed in the United States of America

COUNTERPOINT
2117 Fourth Street
Suite D
Berkeley, CA 94710

www.counterpointpress.com

Distributed by Publishers Group West

10 9 8 7 6 5 4 3 2 1

for Martin

Contents

FOR YOU,
FOR YOU I AM
TRILLING
THESE SONGS

NATURAL'S
NOT IN IT

*T*HE INTENSIVE BRAZILIAN Portuguese class I took at the Boston Language Institute has been a godsend so far. But, perhaps understandably, my lessons have left me lacking the lexicon necessary to convey, in so many words, "Hi, my sister and I would like you to cover our sensitive and never-before depilated pubic regions and butts with molten hot wax and then rip out all the hairs. Yes, please, *all* of them. Thanks!"

Too bad, really, because this is precisely what we'd like to have done. We are in Paranaguá, a medium-sized, totally untouristed port city dozens of kilometers south of São Paulo, and—having been here now almost a month—we've figured, *When in Brazil, why not get a Brazilian wax?*

We are hoping desperately that nobody notices us, sunny mid-morning in this dingy beauty parlor off a cobbled side street. We are the grandnieces of Dom Alfredo Novak, the Catholic bishop, and since few foreigners visit—especially not Americans, especially not Americans related to major and belovéd religious leaders—we are minor celebrities in this town. The other day at a pastry shop, an impeccably coiffed middle-aged woman helped us make proper change to pay for a sticky bun. We didn't think much of it until that night over dinner, when our uncle told us she was the mayor's wife, and that she had called him up to tell him about our encounter. She thought we seemed like such fine young ladies.

We are not being particularly ladylike now. We have resorted, sheepishly at first, and then quite shamelessly, to nonverbal communication, expressing ourselves through a series of hip-height gestures, making emphatic Vs with both hands over our pants, giant arrows pointing, *Here, down here.*

We've spent too much time anticipating this—and too much time looking for a place to have it done—to fail to make ourselves understood. We'd been thinking of just going to the salon in our hotel, but it, like so many things in Paranaguá, is inexplicably closed. So we went out walking, hunting for a place, and chose this one based on its name—*"A Raposa,"* and the stylized fox on its graying awning. Foxy, yes, that's what we want to be.

Beth goes first. I feel like a criminal whose accomplice has just gone off to the gallows without her. I sit flipping nervously through a magazine, the majority of which I can't even read. She comes out not even fifteen minutes later, a naughty smile on her face, and wishes me good luck. "I can't describe it," she says as the stocky woman in charge of intimate waxing leads me back.

The waxing room could scarcely be more sordid and I love it for that. Part of the fantasy is that this is sneaky; this is secret. Nobody but Beth and I know where we are. The mattress looks filthy beneath the crackly white paper, and tiny hairs—which I hope are just Beth's—dust the floor: curly little commas, twisty little question marks. The woman commands me to take off my pants and lay down and I do. The entire episode has the atmosphere of an illicit medical procedure.

A window looks out onto some bleak concrete stairs, stairs which I pray no one will use for the next few minutes or they'll get an eyeful. The windows have no screens, no glass, and the air that rushes in smells smoky mostly, and sometimes salty, sometimes sulphury, blowing across the bay. Beyond the stairs? A fence, the kind of fence we've seen everywhere in Brazil, lined with broken bottles, like stained glass in the sunlight, and atop that, silvery corkscrews of sadistic razor wire.

I'm beginning to think this is an appropriate view, looking as it does the way the pain feels: jagged and shreddy and, I swear, multi-colored. I can barely believe we've chosen to do this willingly. The woman just looks grimly to her work, laughing occasionally when I wince after a particularly ferocious yank. *"Calma, calma."* Be still, she says, but never *Desculpe,* excuse me, I'm sorry. Why would she be sorry? I'm getting what I'm paying for.

She is brusque, efficient, but chattering away. The pain is dizzying and I hardly care about following the conversation. At one point near the end, after a really vicious rip, she holds up the white cloth strip, covered with dark, coarse hairs that until seconds ago had been attached to me, and says with some amusement, some disgust, *"Muito coubertor!"* Very covered! "Yes," I say, "I know." Very covered—that's the whole issue.

It's over in fifteen minutes flat, and then I'm alone again, left to gingerly put my pants back on. When I join Beth out front at the archaic cash register, the woman charges us five reais apiece, the equivalent of about three U.S. dollars. We cannot believe our outrageous good fortune; the cheapness of the procedure helps take out even more of the sting, which is already subsiding.

We are now completely—completely!—clean of hair down there, but we feel pleasantly dirty, mostly because what we've done will remain our secret. We've done something that our uncle and the nuns would be scandalized by. (Well, most of them, aside from Sister Ketty, who went to college in Italy, and who used to race motocross—we suspect she's fairly worldly.) This is something we are certain they would think nice girls don't do. Something with a whiff of *prostituição* about it, a word we heard when the nuns drove us by the notorious motel, Casa Notorna, on our way to help weigh the babies and feed the children in one of Paranaguá's most abysmal slums.

For a second, this makes us feel bad. We are so rich. And we have just spent our money—a small amount, but still, big enough for here—on a somewhat silly indulgence. We try not to walk funny. We look at each other and giggle. When we get back to the Hotel Camboa, we take turns going into the bathroom and checking our newly bare skin in the mirror. We call our fiancés, who will be joining us here soon to get married, and laugh. We've been so good this whole month, and now we've just been slightly bad.

Later that day, our uncle will escort us down to the waterfront, down to the docks where we will catch a small boat to Ilha do Mel, a beautiful and car-less island off the coast. There, in air fresher than any we've ever smelled, we will haul our hairless butts up the steep stairs to the lighthouse and look down at the mist-shrouded sea. We will hike with our new friend, an old friend of our uncle's, Dona Branca, out to Fortaleza, the fort built in 1770 to protect the Bay of Paranaguá from foreign ships. We will look so good, so cute in our sandals, bikini tops, and pants, but it will be a little too chilly to wear bathing suits only. We will wish it weren't the off-season so we could really get bare and enjoy the fact that no hair would ever show.

On one of our hikes along a beach covered with more sand dollars than we've ever seen, I will tell Beth the story of the Victorian art critic John Ruskin on his wedding night, and she will indulge me and listen to the whole thing.

Evidently, although he'd spent his early adulthood up to the age of twenty-eight gazing on flawless nudes by Titian, Veronese, and other Venetian greats, he'd never once laid eyes on the naked body of an actual woman. When the time came for him to do the deed with Effie Gray, he was so horrified by the sight of his new bride's body that he just couldn't do it. Needless to say, poor Effie felt awful, and explained in a letter to her father over six years later that Ruskin had been reluctant to divulge his "true reason" for "not making me his Wife" until very late in the proceedings. As she put it, the problem was that "he had imagined that women were quite different to what he saw I was, and that the reason he did not make me his Wife was because he was disgusted with my person the evening of April 10th."

Meanwhile, in his deposition for annulment, Ruskin stated that "though her face was beautiful, her person was not formed to excite passion. On the contrary, there were certain circumstances in her person which completely checked it." The whole nonsensical affair was cloaked in Victorian modesty, so no one knows for sure, but most scholars conclude that the source of

Ruskin's horror had been Effie's crotch, which was covered—quite naturally, not that he'd have had any way of knowing—in pubic hair.

Of course, the first people we thought of after getting our own pubic hair removed were our soon-to-be husbands, but we knew for sure they already found us "formed to excite passion." We were having a white wedding, but we were not virgin brides. So our sudden interest in waxing was, for the most part, for us—or at least we felt that way.

Back on the mainland, I thought about our secret hairlessness and wondered why we'd waited so long to try it and why we'd tried it at all. On the one hand, we asked ourselves why had it taken us so many years to experience something so fun, so freeing (I mean, bracketing the actual procedure itself)? On the other, we pondered, we had gone twenty-some years with relatively hairy crotches, so what made us decide to get waxed all of a sudden?

I had to admit that I'd originally felt sort of opposed to bikini waxing in general the first time I heard about it, and for many years after that. It struck me as a commodification. A costly and an unnecessary thing. A means of aiding and abetting women in parading around in ever-increasing states of objectified undress. One more source of body anxiety for me as a female person. But since then, I've obviously changed my mind. Not unlike the way I've changed it on other things I used to dislike, such as blogs, the poetry of Wallace Stevens, and Brussels sprouts. Waxing, and specifically Brazilian waxing, has become a thing I don't entirely love (the pain!), but which I mostly like.

Yet it was a sudden shift. Or at least it seemed like it was at first. Thinking back over my past attitudes toward semi-permanent and mildly invasive beauty tricks, it felt now like I'd just tried some hardcore drug without so much as having a drink first. Up until that primal yank at *A Raposa* in August 2005, I'd never even plucked or tweezed. Sure, I'd shaved my legs and armpits. But I'd never gone to a salon to have my eyebrows done. Never been tanning. Never dyed my hair. Never gotten it chemically straightened. I rarely even blow-dried. I was something of a natural woman if you will.

I'd cut my friends' hair, even dyed it in our basement sink in the utility room during junior high, but I'd never undertaken to alter my own appearance so radically. So girl-ily.

I'd been a feminist from an early age, poring over the biography wall at the public library in Woodridge, Illinois, skipping deliberately the Great Men and reading on the Great Women; skipping history and reading herstory: Elizabeth Cady Stanton and Susan B. Anthony. Narcissa Whitman, Lucretia Mott, Julia Ward Howe, Harriet Beecher Stowe, Sacagawea. There was no shortage of heroines for me: Harriet Tubman, Wilma Rudolph, Rosa Parks, Babe Didrikson Zaharias, and on and on. I played with Barbie, but didn't need to be told her crotch and boobs were ludicrous.

In college, I got a bit more aggressive about it, let my hair be its crazy self, cut it super-short, and looked like a pretty boy for a while at the great encouragement of my gay best friend. I rocked the androgyny. Then, after junior year abroad in England, I got into being girly, which is where I am now. I like to revel in my body, and I like to perform femininity. I like to wear "outfits," when possible, as opposed to just "clothes."

That said, it had always been one thing to wear lipstick, but doing anything more permanent remained happily beyond my beauty radar.

In fact, back in civilized Paranaguá after Ilha do Mel, Beth and I find ourselves at a much more reputable salon, run by yet another of my uncle's many good friends. Clean and bright, cheerily staffed and centrally located, this is the place where we are to be washed, styled, and made up before our wedding. The jovial Brazilian woman doing my makeup wants to thin my eyebrows and pencil them back in so that they are *mas bonitas*, more beautiful. Because I am sentimentally attached to my eyebrows just the way they are, I refuse. Deviously, when my eyes are closed for what I think will be shadow and liner, she darts up with her miniature scissors and trims them anyway.

My mother's mother, Granny Marie—the one who gave me my eyebrows—would likely be pleased with this woman's stealth attack, yet scandalized beyond speech were she to know about the beauty procedure she couldn't see. Her eyebrows, with their thickness, their asymmetry—the left one arching archly, and the right one slashing back straight—are mine. I like them on her and I like them on me; they're one of my favorite features, but my grandmother hates them almost as much as she loves to feel guilty, and so delights in blaming herself for this glaring imbalance in my otherwise pleasing face. My vaguely bushy lopsidedness stands in her mind as a minor tragedy, somewhere in there with countless other regrets like not dying young or becoming a nun.

Our other grandmother, Grandma Marge, is more salty. She's the one I got my skin from, pale and clear. I don't see her as much as I'd like, and she couldn't make the trip to Brazil, so Beth and I won't be able to tell her about our new fondness for waxing. But, we decide, we could if we wanted to, if the opportunity came up. We laugh, remembering a couple of years ago, after our grandpa died, when she became one of the most eligible bachelorettes in a cluster of small farming towns in Eastern Nebraska—Waterbury, Walt Hill, Hubbard, even South Sioux City. All the wizened old codgers kept asking her out to Bingo, the Legion Hall, spaghetti suppers and the like, and she told them no. She was enjoying her independence, truth be told, and she couldn't see what could possibly be in it for them. "I don't cook, I don't clean," she explained to Beth and me, "and the other department is closed for business."

Our own mother, who has hovered around like all good mothers-of-brides, helping us with dresses and hairdos and foundational garments, doesn't know we've been waxed, and we won't tell her, either.

She's the reason, partly, I think we didn't get into this sooner. She never paid much attention to our bodies one way or another, nor did she encourage us to do so. Instead, she raised us up like brains in jars. We were always taught, aloud and by example, to locate our worth in our thoughts and actions, not in our appearances. I have early memories of our going to the bathroom together in department stores and gas stations, places where it would have been unwise to let a little girl go off to pee by herself. I remember her own crotch as being big to me—hairy and black—but not scary. Just natural. Just my mom.

Since I've returned from Brazil, Brazilian waxing has become Something I Do, but not terribly often. I've only done it five times total, though the frequency's been inching up slightly. Like lawn maintenance or housekeeping—it's less painful if you do it regularly.

What does it look like, you ask, this Brazilian wax? Excellent question, one which I suppose I should answer. A *full* Brazilian gets rid of everything. Everything! All of it, no hair anywhere. But most Brazilian waxes leave a tiny bit of hair (a triangle, a tuft, a landing strip, whatever you want) above the vulva. To get technical. Since you were wondering.

Being waxed can be hot. Getting waxed is not. The actual process is one of the least sexy things in the world. It's infantilizing. Here is this woman you've just met ministering avidly to your nether parts, using talcum or baby powder, and—depending on the salon—the suggestion of a diaper in the form of the paper thong they might ask you to wear, for modesty's sake. It can also make you feel like a patient in a doctor's office—the high, padded table covered in starchy white paper, the tongue depressors slathered with wax and the gauzy strips of muslin.

My first two waxes back in the States took place in Massachusetts. The first of those was at a salon in Boston where the chipper waxing technician had me don a little disposable G-string, which I found absolutely ridiculous. That time, I was getting waxed for my husband's thirty-fourth birthday. The next time, I did it in Orleans, a small town on Cape Cod, in honor of my own twenty-sixth, and in anticipation of a trip to Austin, where swimming might take place. Again, I was not permitted to be completely naked below the waist, and instead was instructed to fold and hold my underwear as the taciturn year-round Cape Codder worked around it.

Each of these waxes got the job done and was unremarkable, save for their apparent prudery—silly and inefficient. When I'm in the process of getting almost all of my pubic hair forcibly yanked, I don't especially care about modesty, but I complied for the technicians' sake. Maybe it had something to do with the cold New England climate, the puritanical air hanging over those cities, the attendant compulsion toward hiding the dirty.

My fourth time waxing, I was not made to wear undies, but my delight ended abruptly with that dispensation. This particular wax, at a salon in Chicago's West Loop, was the worst one ever.

It had seemed a brilliant idea at the time. I was on my lunch break from my summer job at the office of the senior senator from Illinois. In the grand tradition of office employees everywhere, my coworkers and I were in the habit of stretching our lunches to the limit when they weren't work related. The caseworkers would go to Nordstrom to buy shoes, and our soon-to-be-married press secretary would scope out bridal sales. I spent almost all of mine meeting friends who also worked downtown, and hanging around with Beth who would stop by between photography assignments.

That day, she ate on the El and I ate at my desk so that when we met up in Federal Plaza, we could head straight to the salon. On the way, we talked about how funny it was that so far, 50 percent of the times each of us had been waxed, we'd done it together. That's how close we are; that is one of our bonds. We don't even know if our younger sister does it. We are not close with her.

The salon was uncomfy from the outset. We had an appointment but had to wait and wait, and when we each went back for our respective turns, there was no soothing music, no dim, distracting light—just cheeseball Muzak and bright fluorescents. The waxing woman spoke almost no English, and made me wish urgently that I knew Vietnamese, because I wanted to explain to her that she was *doing it all wrong*, that there was no way something like this should hurt so incredibly and take over forty-five minutes. It crossed my mind at one point to get up and leave before she'd finished, but vanity prevailed and I toughed it out, until only the cutest little tuft of hair was left.

Best not to dwell on the negative, though. Last week I got my pubic hair waxed into a demure yet sassy triangle during what has been, so far, the best wax of my life. Again, the occasion was my husband's upcoming birthday. The second year in a row.

Inconspicuous among a row of shops in downtown Tacoma, the salon, though unisex, is all girly femininity and exaggerated womanhood. Each of the stylists, all female, is made up with heavy foundation, stick-straight hair, militarily perfect highlights, lips with lipstick *and* lip liner. It's like a den of drag queens.

When I tell the girls at the salon—not the women, the girls—that I'm doing this for my husband, they all smile and say how nice, and what a good idea, how sweet. Nobody bats one smoky, fake-lashed eye about how this might be regressive, this might be self-subjugating. That it might be those things even if I don't think it is. That my not thinking it just shows how deeply I'm caught in the trap.

I'm thinking this way because Krystal, the waxer—a lovely distractional conversationalist with a better bedside manner than most doctors I've seen—has just asked me, as I plant myself supine on the table, if I go to school around here.

"Yes I do," I tell her. "In a way." I'm not a student anymore; I'm a professor of English at a nearby small, religiously affiliated university.

She asks if I like Jack Johnson. I don't particularly, but, "Yes," I say. "Good choice. He's so soothing." And he is, he is.

As he plays in the background and an aromatherapy candle burns somewhere on a counter near the foot of the table, Krystal exclaims that I don't look anywhere near old enough to be the teacher, compliments me on my nice long legs, my slim physique. This combination of smells, sounds, and flattery relaxes me. But it also makes me wonder how my fellow feminists among my university colleagues would feel if they knew I was here. Would this be, to them, a huge gender betrayal? An appalling concession to the internalized values of the patriarchy?

I do have evidence to suggest this hair-removal-as-present-to-a-man might upset them. Once, when I was chatting with a superior, I asked about another coworker who was out on maternity leave. "It's not maternity leave. We call it parental leave," she corrected me.

I'm also consistently perplexed by the "partner" phenomenon. On more than one occasion, I've made the mistake of referring to a colleague in a legally recognized and religiously sanctioned heterosexual relationship as a wife, a spouse, or a husband, which apparently people in the academy do not like to be told they are or have, even if they happen to be or have one. It's a reaction that seems illustrative of the weird pretentiousness and imprecision that attend some of the customs of your harder-core academics. "Partner," I'm corrected. So-and-so is my partner. So-and-so and I are partners. Seriously. People get bent out of shape if you screw it up. Clearly, this terminology has a different significance for people in committed same-sex relationships whom Washington law unjustly affords no opportunity to be anything but "partners," but they weren't the ones correcting me.

To a degree, I can understand this. I'm married. I'm a wife. But I haven't changed my name, and this is a decision I made for a very clear feminist purpose. I politely but firmly correct people who call me "Mrs. Rooney." But still. I've talked about the partner appellation with my husband, and he helped me figure out why it makes me feel so ambivalent. He doesn't like the term "partner" as a substitute for "husband" or "wife" because a partnership is an entity that by definition can be dissolved. Marriages can be dissolved too, of course, but the option isn't conceptually built-in from the get-go. Our relationship is more than a business arrangement. It is more than transactional. Or economic. Or work related.

While I'm on the subject of Martin, I should mention that he likes me both ways. Waxed and unwaxed, I mean. He never tries to push me into doing anything I don't want. This, I think, is because he's basically perfect as a person, the closest thing I've seen to a perfect human being. He doesn't drink. He's never had a cavity. Never had a speeding ticket. A stand-up person, a much better person than me, who got my first ticket at sixteen in front of my high school, coming home late, after curfew, trying to get in less trouble and getting in more. Also, interestingly, Martin is impressively unhairy.

My best friend Angela, with whom I went to high school—and who, incidentally, introduced me to Martin while she and I were in college—invented a "make-out code," a handy short-hand for when you wanted to discreetly describe how far things had progressed between you and a boy. If all the action had transpired north of the belt, then you'd remained "loyal to the Union." If things had proceeded south, then you'd "joined the Confederacy."

These are the ways I try to distract myself; these are the thoughts I try to think so I can avoid kicking Krystal in the face, or jerking away when she gently but deliberately—and, I have to remember, entirely at my command—attacks my Confederacy with sickly pink wax.

Krystal, for her part, is bombarding me with engaging banter, telling me how she's almost thirty with a five-year-old son. He's just started school and is a rampant reader already.

"I know I sure wasn't reading at five," she tells me. "Maybe I wasn't a quick learner. Maybe my mom never taught me. Maybe that's why I'm here waxing butts for a living."

For a second I forget about the pain and feel bad.

"Ha!" She says. "Just kidding!" And then, "You don't even realize you have hair in your butt!"

Fun as it is to be talking about butts, we're not there yet, unfortunately. She's done the top and the farthest-out parts of the sides, but now she's moving in, and the pain is excruciating.

She asks, through my pain, if I plan to have kids. No, I say. No way.

"Good," she says. "It seems like you have a low threshold for pain, and it *hurts*."

What you need to know about Krystal, though, the thing that in my mind makes her somewhat heroic—a goddess, an Amazon—is that she gets waxed every three weeks, and above and beyond that, she does it *to herself.* To understand what this is like, imagine poking out your own eye or holding your breath 'til you pass out, and then magnify it to practical self-annihilation, to suicide. Like stabbing yourself in the heart. Like sure, you know that it's possible, and there are people who have done it, but it's virtually impossible to conceive of actually doing it to yourself.

At one point she says, "Don't worry. You still have skin down there. Sometimes I like to mention that, because I've had people ask me."

This is less reassuring than she imagines it is, because until she brought it up, I never doubted that I did. Though it hurts so exquisitely that I wouldn't be surprised.

Krystal is saying, "Don't apologize, you're doing great!"

Jack Johnson is singing, "Sexy Plexi."

Yes, I think. Exactly.

Krystal is saying, "Here, let me pop that ingrown."

Jack Johnson is singing, "She's such a fortunate fool."

Krystal is saying, "Oh, you're bleeding a little."

Jack Johnson is singing, "Hold on if you can."

I can, I think, lying there. *I can, I can.*

The theme of the 101 class I teach at the university is "On Beauty," a subject of my choosing. Recently we read a series of articles on body modification and plastic surgery, including one entitled "The Most Private of Makeovers," about the recent explosion of cosmetic surgery on the female genitals—in hymen restoration, labia contouring, designer laser vaginoplasty, and on and on. This, of course, was the article my singular and extremely sex-positive student Jillian (who in the past has written about modeling panties for her boyfriend—she is brave and a good sharer) hollered out we should discuss when I asked where to start. Derek, the lone male student who had signed up for the class, was conspicuously absent, a move he later admitted was a strategic reaction to the explicit topic of the readings.

My student Rachel, whose day it was to present, stuttered and blushed along with most of the rest of her classmates, and summarized the piece: "It's about women who feel like they need to get beautified, uh, you know . . . down there."

Nervous giggles ran a lap around the conference table as I corrected her, made her say the words. Made them all say the words, for clarity, for precision, and for the sake of owning them: "labia," "vulva," "vagina," and so on.

Why do these women feel the need to do this? we discussed. Why do they play this game of cosmetic modification; this game that runs so counter to what we consider natural? Porn, men, capitalism, they answered, doing my teacherly heart proud.

I told them about the book *Cunt*, and the Riot Grrrl movement, which even I'd been too young to participate in, and which they'd never heard of.

We talked about *The Vagina Monologues*, which all but two of them were embarrassed to even pronounce the name of, and of which some of them had never heard. Jillian, who'd auditioned for it, and Michelle, who was going to be in it, described the show for the class and we discussed its purposes: the raising of funds to prevent violence against women; the raising of pride in our bodies; and more specifically, the raising of awareness about that particular part of the body. But, some of them wondered, why be aware of what's down there?

Michelle and Jillian brought up the fun memorabilia—the vagina pins and vagina buttons, the chocolate vaginas in boxes and on sticks—and I told them about how when I was an undergrad, I'd been able to see Eve Ensler herself perform in the show, and that on the quad we'd had a person-sized papier-mâché vag that you could pose in and get your picture taken.

"You stuck your head through a hole at the top to be the clit," I said.

Karli, an always vociferous student, turned to her pal Dana, her sotto voce more of a basso profundo, and declared, "My teacher just said 'clit'!"

"Yes I did," I said, "and let's talk about why it's a big deal that I did."

"I've never really looked at mine. My vagina. I've never really examined it," said Karli to a chorus of agreement.

"You should give it a shot," I said, and then got back to the article.

My class isn't a consciousness-raising group per se, but I guessed it was good to raise theirs on this issue.

But thinking about it now as Krystal declares, "There. You're almost done. You've been a total champion!" I wonder what it means that I'm lying here thinking about how silly vaginoplasty seems to me—how happy it makes me that it seemed silly also to my students—while getting a Brazilian wax.

But if waxing raises my awareness and pride and pleasure in a part of myself, is that wrong? Is that the Beauty Myth? Is that the triumph of the patriarchy? Is that succumbing, as the article at hand put it, to "aggressive marketing and fashion influences like flimsier swimsuits . . . more exposure to nudity in magazines, movies and on the Internet?" Probably a little. It would be naïve to say that none of those factors play some part in my new affinity.

But here's the thing. Naomi "Beauty Myth" Wolf never said you couldn't wear lipstick. And waxing my pubes makes me like my vagina more both ways, haired and de-haired. Makes me think of its potential, and uses, and how much I like having it. Makes me consider it more. Makes me, as Karli put it, examine it. And isn't that one of the Socratic ideals of the academy? To help you internalize the idea that the unexamined life is not worth living?

Krystal's all done now, and pleased with her handiwork. I'm equally so. While this might not have sounded like a great experience, I should point out that it's the fastest wax I've had in the States. She's rivaled the fifteen-minute duration of the original Brazilian Brazilian, and she gets bonus points for thought-provoking conversation.

She leaves the room to let me put on the after-wax lotion and get dressed, and we've arrived at the part that I like best. Facing the mirror as I slide back into my jeans, it's such a satisfying surprise to look at, to see where once there was hair and now there's not, and to feel the cooling lotion, so exciting and soothing. Icy hot.

I go up front to pay, to get a coupon for five dollars off the next time, and to call Martin to pick me up. For a second I feel guilty again, the way I sometimes do in general for dressing up, but then I'm over it. Fashion is not always pleasant. Glamour is rarely, if ever, natural. To be beautiful can mean to endure pain and to cultivate a dangerous false youth. It can mean you train yourself to follow visual cues we've all been trained to consider hot. But maybe it's okay, even fun, to follow a few of them.

Martin's amazed that I've called so quickly, done already. He's eager to pick me up and see the results.

I don't know what I'm in the process of becoming, don't know where I'm going with this. I just know that I'm going there with very little hair *down there*, at the moment.

FOR YOU,
FOR YOU I AM
TRILLING
THESE SONGS

I WANT TO LIVE in Walt Whitman's America. I want my America "still all in the making." I want it "a promise, a possible something." I want it "an idea, a forecast, a prophecy."

Instead, I live in George Orwell's world. Where "people are imprisoned for years without trial," and "The words *democracy, socialism, freedom, patriotic, realistic, justice* have each of them several different meanings which cannot be reconciled." Where "swindles and perversions" abound. Where "political speech and writing are largely the defense of the indefensible."

◆▷

They say that Nero fiddled while Rome burned. I placed an online order for kazoos while Iraq did. Nero was an emperor. I was a Senate aide.

All the world loves a parade, and I was the girl in charge of ours. I'd been assigned the task of getting our supplies in order for a politician's most important parade date: the 4th of July. Independence Day.

The Declaration of Independence says, "And for the support of this declaration, with a firm reliance on the protection of Divine Providence, we mutually pledge to each other our lives, our fortunes and our sacred honor."

That summer, the summer of 2006, I'd pledged my fortune to working as the assistant internship coordinator in the Chicago office of the Democratic senior senator from the state of Illinois.

That morning, I'd learned from the *Chicago Tribune* that the day I purchased several dozen two-tone red-and-brass kazoos with threaded caps, replaceable resonators, and deluxe tuning was the same day that "a surge of bombings ripped across [Baghdad] and its surrounding provinces killing at least 40 people." Among the dead were the two-man crew of CBS television news correspondent Kimberly Dozier, along with their Iraqi translator and an American soldier.

Ghastly attacks. But what could I do except bracket that, and point and click? Enter the chief of staff's credit card number? Make sure the instruments arrived in plenty of time? Printing out the receipt from Kazoobie, Inc., I stared at the platinum VISA and wondered out loud how the fuck I'd gotten there.

<>

The answer had to do with the fact that I was in the process of making one of the slowest overland, transcontinental journeys since the Oregon Trail.

My husband is a novelist, aspiring but good, and because of his goodness, we'd been living in an artists' colony at a windswept, desolate end of the earth: Provincetown, Massachusetts, in the off-season, when the resort village shrinks from its summer swell of sixty thousand to just thirty-five hundred. Lighthouses. Whales. The Atlantic Ocean. Recluses. Drunks. Gay people. Fishermen. Artists. Writers. Their significant others. My husband was a Fine Arts Work Center Winter Fellow. I shared his bed there. I was a Bed Fellow.

We'd been planning to remain for one more year, but I'd applied for a teaching job at a small religious university in Washington state, and the offer they'd made we couldn't refuse. The fellowship ended the first day of May and the professorship didn't start until the last days of August. With both of us nearly broke, our free housing ending, and rents in Provincetown spiking for the summer, we couldn't just stay there jobless until the fall.

◆▷

So there I was. Back. Working in Chicago. Haunting the suburban town I grew up in like a regressive ghost. I was going west. Manifesting my destiny. In the meantime, I was going a route that is apparently de rigueur among restless twentysomethings everywhere: living with my parents and trying to save money.

I had been an intern myself at the age of nineteen, then a Senate aide at twenty, before I went off to Oxford University, deciding there, dramatically—because I could! I was so young!— that I was actually a poet and always would be. I changed my poli-sci major to English, and put all the petty business of politics behind me.

Of course I hadn't, really. The six years since last I'd worked for the federal government had seemed a second coming of what Gerald Ford termed a "long national nightmare." And though I'd been living in DC during the 9/11 attacks, had marched in 2003 against so-called Operation Iraqi Freedom, and had phone-banked for the Democrats during the heartbreaking 2004 elections, I didn't really see what else I could do to Save the World, to Make a Difference.

Then, staring down the long, cold barrel of a long, hot summer spent in debt in the suburbs, I emailed the chief of staff to see if he might have anything for me in between these bouts of more permanent gainful employment. I wanted, if at all possible, a job that was value-expressive to me—anything more meaningful than temping, retail, or waitressing.

By the time we were done with our lunch, I had a summer gig.

"It will be so lovely to have you back," the chief of staff told me in a basement cafeteria. "Our current intern coordinator can't wrangle all the interns by herself," he added, "and a lot of them can't write the way we need them to. They're college educated, some of them with law degrees, and they can't string together a sentence to save their lives."

That, I was told, would be my main mission. I was so excited, so grateful, that I couldn't even finish my salad. I chose to accept it. "O Democracy, to serve you ma femme!"

◃▹

The mid-May morning I arrived, the elliptical wooden table in the airy glass conference room was ringed with sixteen eighteen-to-twenty-two-year-old faces, most of them substantially less bright-looking than the sun as it glinted on Lake Michigan thirty-eight stories below. Nanette, the intern coordinator whom I was officially to assist, looked somewhat brighter, but completely scattered, disorganized, refracted in a thousand directions, like the light off the water.

I could tell I didn't fit in. And it was not just the fact that I wasn't wearing a suit (though part of the appeal of the life path I'd been on so far—poet and professor—was that I never really *had* to). It had to do with my obvious ambition and enthusiasm. I was temporary, yes, but I did not view this as merely a line on a c.v. or a task to be gotten through, which was more than I would soon be able to say about this crew.

My start date was the same as that of this first batch of interns, and I was as clueless as they were, though I had to fake like I was not. I had to act like the permanent staffers, though all of them clearly knew I was not one of their number either.

I jotted notes on my hand—what I most had to remember. This would come to drive the chief of staff up a tree.

"Kathleen, goddammit," he would say, taking my hand in his and staring down at the ink. "Why don't you use Post-Its like a normal human being?"

What he didn't understand was that this was the only way I could have ready answers to the questions the interns were most likely to ask. I'd have loved for them to demand that I hold forth on political writing and the uses of metaphor, but instead the answers they needed included: "The number to open the voicemail?

Why sure, it's this," and "How do you get in the back door when the front one's locked? With this handy code," and "The password for that computer? Easy, it's . . ."

I did not feel like a fish out of water exactly. And I was not a big fish in a small pond, or a small fish in a big one. I was more like something else that didn't fully belong anywhere. A bird in a pond, maybe.

The summer internships were to be divided in half, into two sessions, imaginatively named Summer Session I and Summer Session II. The only time both cohorts would overlap was at the 4th of July parades, and I was to officiate at this passing of the torch.

For the moment, though, the SSI crew was entirely too large—an absurd sixteen interns for just ten staffers. As we played juvenile icebreaker games (Pick a Starburst! Answer the canned question that corresponds to your color!), they revealed that they possessed the added disadvantage of being the most socially and professionally maladjusted group of people I had ever seen assembled together in one place under the aegis of elitism.

If you selected a red Starburst, you had to name the country you'd most like to visit. "I've already been everywhere I want to go, so I guess I'd say . . . ummm . . . go back to Italy?" said one. If you selected an orange Starburst, you had to describe the most annoying coworker you'd ever had to deal with. "I've never really, like, worked before, so I can't really answer that one," said another. Still another, in response to the orange Starburst prompt, regaled us with a story of working in a gas station with "the meanest butch lesbian on God's green earth," the rest of which was too firmly in the category of Questionable Taste for anyone in her right mind to repeat in polite company.

There has always been some nepotism involved in the fill-ing of political positions. I myself had had an in, back in 1999, because an uncle of mine had worked for the late, esteemed, bow-tied Senator Paul Simon, the current senator's predecessor. I tried to keep this in mind as I met and greeted the members of SSI, but their being there at all was nepo-tastic, out of control. Through a misunderstanding on Nanette's part—you don't *have* to accept everyone, just because some staffer happens to know their moth-er's cousin's best friend's hairdresser—they were almost all hired for their (often tenuous) connections, and not their abilities.

Some of the young charges came from upstate, some from down, and a lot came, like I did, from the middle-class obscurity of the western suburbs. Some came from privilege, some from poverty, but what was evident almost immediately among SSI was that all of them lacked (a) manners, and (b) verbal skills.

◀▶

In "To a Western Boy," Whitman writes:

Many things to absorb I teach to help you become eleve of mine;
Yet if blood like mine circle not in your veins,
If you be not silently selected by lovers and do not silently select
lovers, of what use is it that you seek to become an eleve of mine?

These interns did not want to become eleves of mine. As far as I could tell, they loved little about their positions. They had few passions. But, since it was my job, I did my best anyway.

I wanted to feel awake and alive and I wanted to awaken and enliven them. I could tell, though, that they were suspicious of my background, my teacherhood; they did not understand why I was going to make them read, take them on field trips, and make them write and write and write and write. I think much of the staff shared their suspicion.

Orwell writes: "Modern English, especially written English, is full of bad habits which spread by imitation and which can be avoided if one is willing to take the necessary trouble. If one gets rid of these habits one can think more clearly, and to think clearly is a necessary first step toward political regeneration: so that the fight against bad English is not frivolous and is not the exclusive concern of professional writers." This fight was how (benightedly in hindsight?) I imagined my job.

The chief of staff, I knew, agreed with me; the interns acted like I was giving them busywork, and the rest of the staff felt like I was wasting everyone's time. Why make the interns read Foucault, Lakoff, de Tocqueville, when all they really had to do was alphabetize the files and answer the telephones (tasks which they tackled with the maximum amount of bitching and moaning and the minimum level of speed and competency)?

Orwell's first rule for the improvement of political language states, "(i) Never use a metaphor, simile, or other figure of speech which you are used to seeing in print." If I were to ignore him, I'd say that my interns were the team to my coach or the troops to my drill sergeant, my Bad News Bears or my green recruits. I had to tear them down to build them back up, had to make them over in the image of an ideal—which is to say a thoughtful, well-read, and well-spoken—citizen. I had to teach them to aspire.

Aristotle writes in *The Poetics* that "the greatest thing by far is to have a command of metaphor. This alone cannot be imparted by another; it is the mark of genius, for to make good metaphors

implies an eye for resemblances." The sinister and criminally in-
sane geniuses behind the Bush Administration's war-mongering
and lies—the "Axis of Evil," the "addiction to oil," the "time of
our choosing"—were skilled at metaphors and portentous turns
of phrase and skilled at exploiting them.

So, to better oppose our adversaries, I tried in tiny ways to
encourage our interns to make our own language more lovely and
muscular.

When I was bored at work owing to any substantial amount
of downtime, I sat in my quiet gray cubicle and worked on poems, an activity which connected me to what I saw as my real
life, beyond that summer that had begun to seem increasingly
like an intermission or interlude—short, confusing, removable,
dreamlike.

Despite my affinity for verse, I did not expect my interns to
share it. Poetry per se was not the point of my efforts to expand
their minds. "I have not here been considering the literary use of
language," Orwell writes, "but merely language as an instrument
for expressing and not for concealing or preventing thought."
Exactly. Me too.

Cognitive linguist George Lakoff writes, "Frames are mental
structures that shape the way we see the world. As a result, they
shape the goals we seek, the plans we make, the way we act, and
what counts as a good or bad outcome of our actions. In politics
our frames shape our social policies and the institutions we form
to carry out policies. To change our frames is to change all of this.
Reframing *is* social change."

My mental structures made me believe that making my interns
think equaled a "good outcome" according to Lakoff's logic. I

assigned the interns to read the first chapter of his short and easy-to-understand book, *Don't Think of An Elephant*, then to each pick an issue and try to reframe it using a new metaphor.

I took them by hand and I made them make metaphors. I didn't know if I could reach them. I didn't know if I could teach them. I still don't know if anyone can teach anyone anything. People can learn, but it sort of has to take place on their own terms; they have to want it. I facilitated. I vacillated wildly between thinking my job mattered and thinking it was not worth one single fuck. All the while I kept reminding myself *I am lucky to be here.*

Their reports were, for the most part, boring, half-hearted, and lacking imagination. They were no fun. Aristotle would have disapproved. These people sucked at metaphors. But then again, according to Lakoff so does the whole Democratic Party, though that failed to make me feel much better.

Unfortunately, as with most of my higher order projects during Summer Session I, this wound up being somewhat of a losing battle (sorry, Orwell, forgive the cliché) as I ended up having much bigger—less ambitious but more necessary—battles to fight. Rather than striving to inspire them to push their reframing skills further, I was soon forced to bring them back to basics, including, but not limited to, lowest common denominator standards of courtesy and civil conduct.

◄►

I believe, like my own mom, and her mom before her, that manners might seem small, but they are actually mighty. They are our first best defense against a descent into total barbarism. It is rude not to say thank you in response to a good turn, and it is rude to cut off a fellow driver or to give someone the finger. On a grander scale it is colossally rude to invade a country, for example, in the Middle East, and kill anywhere between 62,144 and 68,141 civilians in the name of "democracy."

Civility comes down to empathy, to the golden rule, to all the stuff we've ever learned about doing unto others. Civility, to me, comes down to my desire to believe that "the main purport of these States is to found a superb friend- / ship, exalté, previously unknown, / Because I perceive it waits, and has been always waiting, latent in all / men," as Whitman describes it in "To the East and To the West."

But even people who do not place such a high premium on politeness would have to fight back the urge to ask my Summer Session I interns whether perhaps they might have been raised by uncivilized wolf-pigs.

I'll spare you the fully itemized list of offenses, but I'll hit the high—low?—lights:

One of our press interns, Steve (nicknamed, for dubious reasons, "The Deuce") had the tendency to sit idly with his wing-tipped feet propped up on the desk in the press cube. The press secretary caught him. I got a talking to and had to give one to him, and had to call a meeting on the importance of, if not staying busy and professional, then at least faking it.

When working reception, Tameka and Nikki did not have the good sense to smile, to say, "How may I help you?," let alone "Hi," to incoming visitors. When they failed to respond to the salutation of Maricela, our Chicago director, one of the nicest people you will ever meet (but also one of the last people you want to mess with in terms of respect), I got a talking to and had to give one to them, and had to call a meeting on the value of speaking when spoken to and putting your best face forward.

When, after the first guest speaker I lined up as part of our Summer Speaker Series, I asked, "Who would like to be in charge of writing the thank-you note?" no one replied. My follow-up— "Who knows *how* to write a thank-you note?"—was met with much avoidance of eye contact and a slight shaking of heads. "What? You people don't have grandmothers?" I gasped before regaining my composure and called a meeting on how to express gratitude to people who have been kind to you.

Daily, the central conference room devolved into a playpen, a rec room. They tossed around the softballs stored in the storeroom for our inter-office league; they hurled magnetized darts against the tall metal file cabinets; they blasted music from lame bands' MySpace pages; and they played tic-tac-toe and hangman on the dry-erase board. They boggled my mind with their lack of propriety; their lack of reverence for the work they were supposed to be doing, for the constituents they were supposed to be helping, and for the people who actually worked there.

◀▶

If Lakoff is correct, and the best metaphor for understanding politics in America is that of the family, then we, my Summer Session I interns and I, were seriously dysfunctional. I was the well-meaning single mom, they were the punkass recalcitrant kids, and everyone else was an absentee father. My nurturing approach was being thrown into serious doubt by their increasing demand for punishment and tough love.

My coworkers silently and not so silently began to blame me for the interns' rudeness and indomitability. Maricela asked, wisely, that we have them write their own letters of recommendation, in the hope that by attempting to catalogue what they had accomplished they would realize they had done perilously close to nothing and get their asses in gear. The press secretary wanted a contract, a piece of paper outlining duties and requirements that all the interns would have to read and sign so there could be no more excuses.

The hot June day I went to draw the contract up, the news was filled with reports on recently approved changes in the Latin-to-English translation of the Catholic Mass. I had not been to Mass regularly in years, but the words remained engrained in my brain. The chief of staff—also Catholic, also semi-lapsed—and I debated the value and impact of these updates over lunch.

"In an accompanying comment section, some bishops wrote anonymously that the new wording was 'very awkward' with a 'heavy, ponderous and often turgid style' that uses 'irregular, passive and run-on sentences'," I read aloud from the newspaper lying on the break-room table. "Others, however, said they favored the new translation because it was more poetic and beautiful, more accurate and more faithful to the Latin version."

"Of course they've played up the old guilt aspect," the chief of staff cracked, grabbing the paper and reading, "And instead of confessing, 'I have sinned through my own fault' during what's called the penitential rite, Catholics would say, 'I have sinned greatly . . . through my fault, through my fault, through my most grievous fault.'"

I was feeling fairly guilty myself, grappling with how best to make an effective contract for the interns.

"I'm happy they left the part of that prayer about sinning 'in my thoughts and in my words, in what I have done, and in what I have failed to do' alone. I've always liked that passage," I said.

"You're really into those sins of commission and omission, aren't you Kathleen?" he asked, raising his eyebrows and biting his sandwich.

I supposed I was.

Back at my cube I added to the wording of the contract that interns were not merely to do what they were directly asked, but also to avoid the mistake of sitting around and doing nothing; they were neither to commit any questionable acts, nor to neglect to make sure that they were, in fact, doing all that they possibly could.

My fixation on commission and omission had to do, I decided, with my own sense that perhaps I was not doing enough to Save the World. True, à la the Hippocratic Oath, I was first doing no harm. I was trying not to actively commit any grievous sins against my fellow humans. But perhaps I was leaving out—omitting— some essential actions that could make the world better. I was definitely not performing up to my own standards at my allegedly value-expressive and politically engaged job.

The behavior of my interns baffled and depressed me. As was my wont, I blew the situation up to the nth degree. I began think- ing about how manners are the basis of the social contract, and how if you don't follow that, everything goes out of whack. Of course I knew that Steve's feet up on the desk was not an act of terrorism and that Tameka and Nikki's failure to say hi was not tantamount to an imperialist invasion of an entire country, but their behavior made my job really hard, and me really sad.

"I will plant companionship thick as trees along all the rivers of / America, and along the shores of the great lakes, and all over / the prairies," writes Whitman in "For You, O Democracy." Yet many were the days during Summer Session I that I felt companionless—paranoid, alienated, more *1984* than *Leaves of Grass*.

Stop obsessing, I told myself, whenever the interns got too ridiculous to bear. *Think about all the other stuff you're good at.* And it was true. I hadn't just been hired to make the interns better writers; I'd also been hired to write myself. My political language never defended the indefensible. I wrote letters to the editor. I wrote press releases. I wrote congressional proclamations and letters of congratulations commemorating people on their life achievements: one-hundredth birthdays, fiftieth wedding anniversaries, careers as educators, figures in the arts, and leaders in the nonprofit sector.

Still, I couldn't help but spend the humid days thinking about the relationship between politics and poetry, between work and love, between beauty and utility, and whether these pairs must always be uneasy bedfellows. Whether there wasn't some way to transform hopes into actions, to communicate a dream into some kind of reality. As June slunk onward, I remained in that in-between state, a cracked-up mash-up of politics and poetry, which was not just a side product of my work, but which was encouraged by the chief of staff.

"You're a smart girl, Kathleen," he said. "You'll figure something out."

I reminded myself that, in fairness, there were simply too many of them, way too many for this around-the-office stuff to be going smoothly. It was becoming clear that the parade on that now not-too-distant 4th of July—if for no other reason than their high numbers—might be my shot at redemption and their one time to shine.

I clung to this hope because in my weakest, most frustrated, and most claustrophobic moments—times when I felt I would never leave the office, that I was incompetent, that their bad attitudes were somehow not their faults but mine—it seemed like all I had. I set up a parade committee staffed by interns, and subdivided that into subcommittees, each with an area of focus and expertise: food, music, transportation, T-shirts, decorations, and favors to throw. The chief of staff was such a cheapskate that in the end, we were allotted almost no money to actually acquire any of these items. The food would come from a free barbecue organized by a local Democratic organization, we would wear last year's T-shirts, and carry the same banners we'd carried every year since the senator had been elected.

"I want whatever junk we toss to cost no more than a nickel, and we sure as hell aren't hiring any kind of band," the chief of staff told me when we discussed our parade budget.

"You're going to have to throw nickels then, because according to Nikki and Tameka's research, even the cheapest stupid paper fans cost thirteen cents each. And as far as music goes, what do you want me to do? Teach them to sing?"

And that was how I ended up ordering three dozen kazoos. We wouldn't have to throw anything, and we'd have instant music if every intern was handed an instrument and told to play, the chief of staff concluded in a feat of logic that confirmed, again, why he was a brilliant chief of staff.

The interns were delighted. Kazoos! Kazoos! The break room was abuzz—at first, metaphorically, and when the shipment arrived, literally. The parade subcommittees killed their time for slacking, and got them finally—finally!—excited about something.

In my dark nights spent wondering whether I was really *doing* anything, wondering whether the notion of *making a difference* might be, in my life at least, no more than a myth, I thought about the kazoos and the parade and how the senator would be there and how maybe we would all be one big happy democracy.

◆▷

Once, discussing our framing projects, Nikki sighed out loud that "Writing is hard. Metaphors are hard."

"I agree," I said. "But why do you say that?"

"Because I have this perfect idea in my brain and in my heart of how things should be, and when I try to get it down it won't come out that way."

A nod of agreement ran in a wave around the table, and we all had a chat about the inevitable loss between idea and execution. About the frustration that occurs when we go from promise to actuality, from prophecy to reality, and how you can never say whatever it is you want to say exactly the way it seems in your mind.

That afternoon I was happy and the parade crept closer.

The parade would be a cavalcade of all I'd done, like a talent show, a quiz bowl, a spelling bee. The interns and I would all show up and perform and everyone would see we'd finally made something of our sorry selves.

◂▸

When the day finally arrived, it felt at first like an underdog-wins-in-the-end movie where the underdog would never win in real life. Like the script was a joke, all the actors miscast. I wanted to be a hero, but was playing a fool.

As we piled into the rented minivans downtown—the interns from Summer Session I, the new ones from Summer Session II, and the staffers—I stared at the interns in their yellow-and-blue senior senator T-shirts clutching their shiny kazoos and wondered if maybe I wasn't kidding myself about our heading toward some kind of salvation for the previous six weeks.

We arrived at the first parade in Wheaton, Illinois, a conservative suburb in conservative DuPage County, twenty-five miles west of Chicago. The home of Wheaton College, the alma mater of evangelical preacher Billy Graham, Wheaton contains forty-five churches, reputedly more per square mile than any other U.S. City.

Tragedy enobles. Comedy cuts down to size. What else could this job—this day—be, but both? I thought.

The chief of staff—after all this stress and preparation—was away with his family at his home in Springfield. But the senator was with us, and as we began to march under the lurid sun, in the middle of the lineup, after the brassy marching bands, the sequined major-ettes, and the howling fire trucks, he was marching beside me.

"It's the poet!" he said, smiling, avuncular. "Have you got any patriotic poetry to recite?"

I am a terrible memorizer, but the man was a senator. "O Captain, My Captain!" I declaimed, because Abraham Lincoln is very important, and Illinois is the Land of Lincoln; this land is his land, even if he was a Republican. Also, "O Captain, My Captain!" and "She Walks in Beauty Like the Night" by Byron are about the only poems I know by heart (besides my own) and of those it's certainly the more patriotic.

Once I finished the first stanza and the senator had moved ahead to kiss the babies and press the flesh, I inquired of my kazoo-bearing interns, "Do you take requests?"

"You bet," said Matt.

"My Country 'Tis of Thee?" I tried. And to my disbelief, they complied. Not only that, but they complied with zeal and panache. The "1812 Overture," "America the Beautiful," and "Stars and Stripes Forever" followed in quick succession, and they kept up their improbable music for the duration of the mile-and-a-half course.

At the end of the route, the senator, surrounded by kazooing interns, made his way through the people lining the roadside until he got to a dour and balding man in a "Roskam for the House" T-shirt. The senator reached out to shake his hand, but the man pulled it away, his face a rictus of disgust. The senator recovered gracefully, petting the head of the dog at the man's side, but the man jerked the animal back.

"My dog is Republican, too," he snapped.

And in a feat of kazooing that could have brought a tear to even the driest eye, the interns responded to rudeness with big-hearted kindness and humor. Matt had them strike up "The Battle Hymn of the Republic." And it didn't matter that the parade would soon end, that the Republican candidate would win this seat, that I would move away to Washington state, and that the interns would go on to other internships, other places to pad their resumes. For a moment, we'd done it. We were in Whitman's America.

Sun-drenched and sweaty in their Senate regalia, kazoos in their right hands, cheap vinyl American flags in their left—they bore the senator along: "the party of young fellows, / robust, friendly, / Singing, with open mouths, their strong melodious songs."

FAST ANCHOR'D,
ETERNAL, O LOVE!

*O*NCE UPON A time, there was a girl who got everything she wanted, but was still unsatisfied.

Well, not everything. Maybe just everything she asked for, or rather, everything in her power to ask for directly.

She was a newlywed, and she and her belovéd were between jobs, between coasts, paused on their way from Provincetown, Massachusetts, that spring to Washington state in the fall. They both needed work to do in the meantime.

The last thing she wanted was to spend the summer idle in her parents' basement in Illinois, though she did end up spending it under the (very) watchful eye of a man their age.

◀▶

She took the train downtown to see an old friend, to see about a job. This old friend, her once and future boss, reached across the grainy beige cafeteria table in the tiny booth they were sharing in the Bank of America building in the Chicago Loop. He helped himself, with her plastic fork, to bites of the salad he'd bought her that she was too wound up to finish. They talked about what she was going to do with herself those three sunny months, and whether it would involve her doing something for him.

Turns out, it would. She'd do office things—organizational and low-level administrative—and look after the interns. She would spend a lot of time sitting around looking pretty, which isn't the worst thing one can do for a living, all things considered.

◂▸

Her friend Mary Beth who went to high school with her in the depressively named town of Downers Grove, nineteen miles west of the Windy City, says the best reason to get married is so you can eat food off your spouse's plate.

◂▸

Little-known fact she shared with her once and future boss at lunch: the Pilgrims landed at Provincetown before they rocked Plymouth. He had always been an ambivalent patriot and a bit of a history buff and was interested, casually, in such casual trivia.

◂▸

Well-known fact often touted as little-known: Chicago is called the Windy City not for its weather, but for its politicians, blustery windbags, suit-clad, all pumped to the gills with campaign promises—so much hot air.

◂▸

Little-cared-for fact: Tacoma, Washington, is known as the City of Destiny, western terminus of the Northern Pacific Railroad, way down deep on south Puget Sound: where rails meet sails.

◆▶

Little fact cared for a lot by her: her once and future boss (the chief of staff) and his boss above him (the senator) both loved rails—sons, as they were, of railroad men.

The chief of staff also loved sails, ships, and Canada; she did too. These are facts that she will always remember. These are facts that will be important later.

◆▶

She did not set out to become a favorite, but she became the favorite just the same.

Her once and future boss loved to say her name and would say it over and over, all the time, would call her into his office, huge and central in the suite of blue and gray cubicles, an actual room with a massive wooden desk, a black leather sofa, and a spectacular view of the lake and skyline. Ships and boats, silver in the sunlight, would cut across the water like scissors through blue fabric.

Sometimes, he would need her to take care of a project—to write a letter, a press release, a proclamation, or to give her opinion on some pressing issue. Other times, he just wanted to talk. "Have a seat," he would say, and she'd sink into the cushions, and then he would say her name and tell her a story. He would say something funny and she would laugh, then she would say something funny back and he would do the same.

◀▷

Once upon a time, there was a girl in unrequitable (but not unrequited) love with her boss.

Every day she would dress up and every day he would compliment her on it. "Do you like wearing that skirt?" he might say the day she wore her pale and crisp-ribboned crinoline, frothy as a summer drink. "Yes," she'd say. "Why?" "I can just tell by the way you wear it."

She was not a princess. But that is what he called her.

◀▷

She was so lonely sometimes, she thought something must be wrong with her.

"We read to know we are not alone," said C. S. Lewis in a book she was reading. She read a lot anyway, but she read even more than usual that summer, always on the train in the morning and at night. The ride was like a chapter, with the beginning and the ending switching places depending which way she was headed: sometimes the story started in Downers Grove and wound up in Chicago, sometimes the opposite. Sometimes she was the heroine, sometimes she was no one.

◀▷

Because the office was overstaffed, lousy with interns, she was not exactly awash in jobs to do. She'd wrap up her real work in a matter of hours, and—no more being forthcoming—she would find herself facing an expanse of downtime, during which she would write, one of the things she did normally, in her real life, the life not spent working for her boss.

He'd come into her cubicle, sit down behind her. At first she'd try to look busy, to hide what she was doing, but he didn't care, he didn't mind—in fact he even liked it.

"I didn't think we had much of a call for poets in our office," he said. "But I can admit when I've been wrong."

He would place his hand at the base of her neck, or flick her earring, or twist a strand of her hair. He might tell her about some book he'd been reading; he read all the time too, though she couldn't guess whether he felt lonely. He would touch her shoulder; he would wander away.

He ran the office this way—on the ragged edge of decency. He was the Lord of Misrule, blue eyes always with a lurid gleam, but also an edge of something smart and hard, something meaner, that he kept mostly in check. He kidded around—teasing the scheduler, mocking the press team, screaming at people—goddammit they were useless!—but with total affection. He would screech like a nail coming out of a board when he was outraged, which was often, but he asked her on more than one occasion, when she feared she'd screwed up, "Have you ever seen me angry? Really angry?" No, she had not.

McCarran, the guy in the cubicle behind hers, would greet her boss in kind: "You gain a few pounds over the weekend? Cuz the asshole suit seems to be fitting a little tight."

Gap-toothed, smirking, her boss would punch McCarran in the arm, call him a pansy, and wave him into his office to discuss the day's business.

<>

She was a nostalgic dresser. Her clothes expressed emotions. One day, she wore the ones she'd been wearing the very first time she'd met her boss's boss, at a constituent breakfast at the Capitol during a high school trip to Washington DC: a skirt to mid-calf, tiger eye earrings, and a gauzy silk scarf around her neck, her long dark hair swept up and back. A man impressed by both thrift and discipline, her boss had been immensely pleased that she could, ten years later, wear clothing she'd worn as a student, that she'd neither gained weight, nor gotten rid of the outfit.

Standing in her cubicle, rubbing the ends of the scarf between his fingers, he marveled to one of her coworkers, an older woman about to retire, "Can you believe that she's the same size she was when she was sixteen?"

"Tell me how," he said, and said her name, "how do you manage, always, to look so damn ssss . . ." The S hissed like air escaping a tire. Ssssexy. Sexy, he'd been going to say, but that, according to the rules of harassment posted in the break room, would have been imprudent. ". . . sssssmart," he wrapped it up. "How do you manage, always, to look so damn smart?"

"This scarf?" she replied. "Actually, it holds my head to my neck. If I didn't have it on, my head would fall off."

"Smartass," he smiled and strode away.

◀▶

She tried to be virtuous, perfect, pure of purpose. She had wanted this job in the first place because she wanted to help Save the World.

She tried to tell her boss that, to show it with her actions, and she always worked extra hard at the few tasks that were her responsibility.

"I want to take care of that mess in Iraq," he would say, and

"I want the good guys to win in the mid-terms," and

"I want to run away with you in that dress."

Her boss did not always get what he wanted, though he was a direct man and asked directly.

◀▶

Sometimes, riding the train in the early evening, she would try to uproot his face and transplant him. The air outside was muggy, but in the cars it was conditioned, cold, and she got goose bumps on her upper arms, her thighs, as they barreled through the suburbs, bricky and dirty at first, then leafy and green by the time she got home.

Would I still be so attracted if he were not the boss that he is, but a bum on the bus? He might be ravished, rugged, slavish, drugged, but yes, still handsome. But would he be less appealing? Less witty? Less charming? Or still those things? As her train neared the stop, she would decide this was silly. He would not have the job he did if he did not have the personality.

◄►

Her boss was dapper, though not a dandy—oxblood shoes, bespoke trousers, tailored jackets, and white linen suits. Natty but manly. He was always cool, smooth, dry, even when other men's shirts went dark under their arms, when their faces went dark with five o'clock shadows.

His appearance seemed to match both his job and its importance. His job and its power, his job and its luxury.

She'd bring in letters she'd written for him to sign, the stationery bleached and white as his collars, crisp as his cuffs, embossed at the top in raised glossy ink with a government seal, blue as the lake.

He lived in a hotel with high threadcount sheets and soft cotton towels. He was a discriminating man, a man of taste.

◄►

The feeling she got whenever they talked was like a strong narcotic, precise in its effect. She was constantly afraid of somehow wrecking everything, of disappointing him, of not having the right outfit, the right writing, the right clever comeback.

◄►

She expected a lot from people. From life. She was often disappointed. Her husband told her he was impressed by the way she could never manage to hope for the best and expect the worst. She only ever got that advice half right, the first half, and was continually let down, down, a bucket in a well, a ship taking on water, then bailing, bailing.

Her husband seemed to imply—gently; he was the kindest man—that this was a mark of immaturity, that she'd outgrow it eventually. She half-believed him. But one day, on her commute, she read an essay that said,

> disappointment is the flip side of a strong, predictive feeling for beauty or appropriate civility or decency: only those with a sense of order and harmony can be disappointed. If we continue to expect what turns out to be not forthcoming, it is not because we are unworldly in our expectations, but because our very worldliness has taught us to demand of an unjust world that it behave a little more fairly. The least we can do, for instance, is to register the expectation that people in a stronger position be kind and not cruel to those in a weaker one, knowing all the while that we will probably be disappointed.

Underemployed though she often felt, she didn't think she could do the job she was doing—trying to help people, to provide them services to improve their lives—if she didn't still have this capacity for deep disappointment.

◂▸

Her boss's behavior, her friends told her, should probably have disappointed her, a man in his position taking such obvious advantage of his power, but she didn't see it that way. "There's a really big difference," she'd try to explain, "between harassment and play. It's all just a game. And at the end of the day, I have as much power over the situation as he does." She was pretty smart, most of the time.

She told her husband about her boss, and he said it was okay, no big deal, he was fine with it. He quoted her something from Lacan, from Barthes, about how the frisson had to do with language and wit and power and games. Her husband worked in a bookstore. He was writing a novel. He owned more books than anyone she had ever met and one of them happened to be Barthes' *The Pleasure of the Text.* "Barthes says all reading passes through a dilatory space between the beginning and the ending, and that is what creates the pleasure, what creates the pull, the suspense. The tension is maintained through deferral and postponement. The pleasure of this space—of this game—is based on implication and suggestion but with no resolution. Suspension and anticipation propel the experience, but it never concludes."

"What do you mean?" she said, staring at his profile in the driver's seat, in the late golden light, as he drove back to her parents' house from the train station.

"Your boss isn't looking for consummation—it's the constant frustration, the pleasure of deferral." He was really smart, pretty much all the time.

"So this summer is like a book, and I'm like the girl in the book."

"Sure," said her husband. "You're like the girl in the book."

◂▸

Her boss also had "a strong predictive feeling for beauty or appropriate civility or decency." He had a finely honed "sense of order and harmony."

So did many visitors who came into their office. Many of them were protestors. Many of them thought that by lying down on the floor and pretending to be dead—as dead as the civilians and soldiers being killed every day half a world away—they could end the war. This was a nice idea. But this was not the case. Her boss and her boss's boss were both against the war, but the boss above everyone, the commander-in-chief, was for it, and so it went on.

Her boss hated it when the protestors showed up, not because he disagreed with them, but because they created disorder and disharmony. Once, when there were pretend-dead people sprawled all over the blue carpet in front of the reception desk, her boss said her name, called her into his office.

"Could you please do me a favor?" he said.

"Depends what you're about to ask," she said, not looking at him, but out the floor-to-ceiling glass at the lake, at the boats.

"Could you please call building security and get those people removed?"

"No," she said. "Sorry. I won't."

"I didn't think so," he said, not without respect. He waved her away wearily; he picked up the phone.

<>

Her boss was what some might call, politely, a lover of women—the ordered and harmonious ones anyway. He openly admired them. He had no shame. She tried not to act jealous— why should she be? She was married. Happily. It was none of her damn business—but her heart twisted slightly, like a corkscrew, every time he opined about another woman's beauty.

He got his hair cut in the neighborhood every few weeks, and he was always giddy on the days of his appointments. His haircutter worked at a cheap barbershop during the day and at Hooters at night. It was her understanding that this woman gave excellent haircuts. In addition she had huge boobs and tons of tattoos.

◀▶

Her boss was also harsh in his abuse of women he considered ugly (men too, though this never depressed her as much). Never to their faces, always behind their backs—real women or famous ones—he would disparage them for being manly, fat, wrinkled, or badly dressed.

One day in the break room, she was reading a review of a play about the life of Golda Meir. Her boss had come in for some coffee, peered over her shoulder and said that to his memory, Golda had been part of a time in world history when it was like an international race to see which country could come up with the ugliest female leader.

She had replied that the male officials back then—and now for that matter—were not exactly prize specimens, nor were looks really the point, but he'd gone off whistling, mug in hand.

◀▶

As the summer wore on, as it drew closer to time for their story to end, for her and her husband to move away, her boss seemed petulant, pouty, a truculent little kid.

Her younger sister lived in the same big city. They often had lunch together. They would meet in the plaza below her tall building and sit outside, watching the people, the pigeons, the market. They'd visit vendors for dessert, asking for damaged fruit they could have for free. Vendors giving her things made her boss jealous. And she liked it.

"Invite your sister up sometime," he'd say, as she finished a free apple or a free pear or a free peach. "I'd love to meet her."

So one day she did.

"You seem very nice," he said, kissing her sister's hand. "Which is a bit of a surprise, frankly, because your sister's kind of a bitch. She has a terrible attitude."

"I hear you're kind of a bitch yourself," her sister smiled back.

"Well, now, that may be true. Look, I don't know why I keep her around in the first place, but you know she's breaking my heart by going away."

◆▷

He was older than her, twice as old, and he had children, all grown up. He had a daughter her age, and he made a point to introduce them to each other at a fabulous event. This made her sad. She didn't know why, or rather she wouldn't say. She made small talk as her boss wandered off, but she and the blonde girl didn't have all that much in common. After a few minutes, she knocked back her gin and tonic, then excused herself and went back to the bar.

◀▷

Sometimes, she'd feel frustrated over the way her job was going. It was so small to begin with and when something went wrong, it would make her want to quit. He'd call her into his office.

"Shut the door," he'd say.

"Okay." She did.

"You know I adore you."

"Yeah," she said. "Though I can't imagine why."

"Now wait, goddammit. You're supposed to say, 'That's all that matters.'"

"That's all that matters," she said, lacking conviction, the sad voice of a sad actress.

"Now say it again, this time with feeling."

And she would and she'd feel better in spite of herself, light as the buoys bobbing out in the lake.

◀▷

She read a little Barthes on the train one day. "Herein a great enigma, to which I shall never possess the key: Why is it that I desire So-and-so?" wrote the dead French man.

> Why is it that I desire So-and-so lastingly and long-ingly? Is it the whole of So-and-so I desire (a silhouette, a shape, a mood)? And in that case, what is it in this

loved body which has the vocation of a fetish for me?
What perhaps incredulously tenuous portion—what
accident? The way a nail is cut, a tooth broken slightly
aslant, a lock of hair, a way of spreading the fingers
while talking, while smoking? About all these *folds* of
the body, I want to say that they are *adorable*. *Adorable*
means: this is my desire insofar as it is unique: "That's
it! That's it exactly (which I love)!" Yet the more I experience the specialty of my desire, the less I can give it
a name [. . .] Of this failure of language, there remains
only one trace, the word "adorable."

◀▶

This is the story of a girl who got her picture taken with a
Mountie.

She took the interns down to Daley Plaza for lunch because
she was tired of them buying fast food and schlepping it back to
the break room to eat in front of C-Span. She wanted to show
them the farmers' market, the international festival, the beautiful
city. Boring and fat, they were unimpressed, but she and her sister
had a lovely time.

You could see it in the photograph: the strapping Mountie
grinning, clutching a handful of her hip.

"Boy, that guy sure has got a grip on you, doesn't he?" her
boss remarked grimly when she came into his office to give him a
small red plastic maple-leaf lapel pin. She had also taken one to
bring home to her husband.

"You like Canada?" he asked.

"Yes."

"Why?"

"I don't know. The romantic allure of the Great White North? The manners? The Quebecois?"

"Yeah, me too, and I don't know why either. But there are a couple of events coming up that I'd like you to come to. As my guest."

◁▷

The first event was a fundraiser for a female war hero running for office. It was put together in part by a prominent Democratic feminist whose father had built his empire by publishing glossy color pictures of naked women with platinum hair and enormous breasts. He liked to compare women to animals, specifically to the soft and fluffy long-eared kind, cute and cuddly and fond of sex.

The second event was the opening party of the Tall Ships Festival, during which dozens of ships in full sail and regalia would be docking in the Chicago River and the Lake Michigan harbor. Her boss had been invited to a dockside reception in honor of the captains and crews of the three from Canada: the *Pathfinder*, the *Playfair*, and the *Barque Picton Castle*.

◁▷

The fundraiser was first. She stuck around the office later than usual that night, bored and excited to get on the road. When she returned from freshening up in the boss of her boss's private bathroom, her boss clapped, thumbsed up, and said, "A-plus. You look like a million bucks."

They drove north from the Loop in a Jeep, Kathleen riding shotgun and her boss in the back. The Jeep belonged to and was driven by a man named Tim, one of their colleagues from another office in the black Mies van der Rohe building. His boss was eventually going to run for president.

The event was both more and less glamorous than it might seem from the outside, held in a luxury apartment with a grand view of the Swissôtel and the green Chicago River.

The food was marvelous, small and nouveau: mascarpone cheese atop figs atop curried shortbread, a Christmas cookie taste in late July; potato samosas with mint and cilantro—spicy, but in a sheet of pastry reminiscent of a McDonald's apple pie; delicate sushi with avocado, wasabi, and ginger.

Once glasses of white wine were clutched in both her hand and Tim's, her boss asked the hostess—a fashionable woman of a certain age—where the deck was. She corrected them, "It's not a deck, I'm afraid; it's a terrace."

At first she was annoyed at what she perceived as the woman's snobbishness, but when they stepped out, she appreciated the precision; the space was expansive, practically Roman. The woman was right; it really was a terrace. The river smelled like piss. Being slightly tipsy helped her think this. It began to rain.

Back inside, they had a coppery green set of high-powered binoculars aimed across the river at the fish tank windows of an elegant building that she couldn't identify. She was sure her boss would know, but he had gone off to mingle with other men and women his own age, leaving her to talk with Tim.

"Where's your boss?" she said to him as it got later, almost time for the female war hero to speak. Tim's boss was supposed to do her introduction.

"To everyone else, he's somewhere really important and can't break away," said Tim, leaning in. "Between you and me, he's at the gym."

This revelation disheartened her, but "Cool," she said. "If you're going to run for president, you've got to be in shape."

"Exactly," said Tim. "I should go call him."

She downed her wine, got a refill, and sat on a plump taupe sofa in the room where the female war hero was going to speak. Her boss came in and sat down next to her.

"It's about ten degrees cooler in here," he said, looking at the side of her face. "You know, it's been a joy to have you here this summer. I hate that you're leaving. I can't wait to see you again. I can't wait to see you in five years."

"I don't want to get old," she said.

"No, you'll look great. Women get better with age."

"Really?" she replied. "Orwell said that by the age of fifty, every man has the face he deserves."

Her boss was fifty-six. Her boss made a face.

The room got crowded and the crowd got quiet. The female war hero stood with a cane. She had no legs. She was thirty-six. She lost her lower limbs in the war, in a helicopter accident during which she saved both herself and the troops with her. The female war hero was smart and sincere. She said the best thing she learned from the Army was how to speak truth to power. After her speech, she sat down for the Q&A.

She made statements that would have sounded melodramatic from anyone with less ethos. But the female war hero made them quietly with conviction. "We had steak and lobster every night at the war," she explained. "But I would have eaten dog food—I would have eaten garbage if only I could have had the proper armor for my kids."

And everyone in the room believed her, for they knew it was true. *My kids, my kids*—that's what she called her troops. The female war hero made her into an active listener. She nodded, agreed, got tears in her eyes. Her boss did too. He sniffled once, discreetly, beside her.

Afterward, her boss introduced her to the finance manager for the female war hero's campaign. "I've heard your name," he said, smiling at her, an obvious lie. She got to shake the hand of the man who would one day soon be running for president too, but all the rest of the evening's handshakes were nothing compared to that of the female war hero.

People kept saying they were pleased to meet her, kept telling her she should stick around for a while, but her boss was leaving, and she decided to go too. The evening would not get any better than hearing what the female war hero had said, and she opted to get out before she wound up disappointed.

Back on the street, she felt simultaneously triumphant and defeated. The sun had come back out to set. It was still light, but her boss insisted on walking with her until she found a cab. He handed her a twenty and saw her safely inside.

"What will you do with the rest of the night?" she asked him.

"None of your damn business."

"Oh, is it that exciting?"

"I'm going to go home and read. Raymond Chandler. *The Long Goodbye.*"

"Goodbye," she said. "Goodbye, goodbye."

◁▷

"Did you have a good time at the fundraiser?" her boss asked, and said her name.

"Yes. She's wonderful. Too wonderful. I don't think she'll win."

Her boss didn't like that. He changed the subject.

"How do you manage to look so good all the time, especially on what I pay you?"

She said his name, and then she said, "What is it like to be so full of bullshit?"

Outside, the lake sparkled blue beneath a white serpentine of ships. It was the first day of the festival. It was the Parade of Sail.

◁▷

Some little-known facts about the Tall Ships reception that warm Thursday night in early August on the breezy banks of the Chicago River:

Her boss was the special guest of the Canadian consulate; she was the special guest of her boss. When he pinned her nametag to her plunging neckline, he joked, "No matter what you do tonight, you'll look like a boob."

Canadian Mounties wear beautiful boots. But according to the one they spoke to (because, she knew, this Mountie was female and cute), civilians are not permitted to order or wear them.

J. P. Cormier is world-renown singer from Nova Scotia. He provided the evening's entertainment at an open-air stage, the blue-green river behind him.

A white-blonde woman with ice-blue eyes from the mayor's office kept staring at them coldly. "I think she thinks it is unbecoming of a man like me to be out and about with the likes of you," said her boss.

There were many white tents set up along the banks, as well as black plastic mesh for the guests to walk on. If you stepped off, the banks were muddy and treacherous. Her boss discovered this at a weak spot in the mesh, his foot dropping through, his ankle twisting. It immediately began to swell and turn purplish-blue. "Oh my god," she said. "Are you okay? Do you need to go home?" "It hurts like a bitch," he said. "But no. I'm having too much fun to go home. In fact, maybe this is a curse for my having too much fun. With you."

The Consulate General of Canada contains a lot of nice middle-aged men with Irish last names and well-kempt mustaches. Three of these immediately circled around them to make sure that her boss was, in fact, okay. As two of them helped him to a chair and fetched a bag of ice to ease the swelling, one remained behind and apologized to her: "I'm so sorry about what happened to your husband—we'll have to fix that walkway.

But we appreciate his being so good-natured about it." Feeling strange, she decided it was easier not to correct the nice man. She also decided not to tell her boss; it is easier, perhaps, to keep some facts to oneself.

◁▷

After the reception, neither of them wanted to go straight home. Leaning on her for support, he asked her what she'd like to do next. "I'd say get another drink, but you don't drink," she said. "Why don't you?"

"I don't drink now because I used to drink. Once I drank everything. I drank it all."

They stopped and bought a pack of cigarettes instead and smoked them on a bridge, leaning over the railing, exhaling toward the river and the lights of the city. She wondered how the two burning cherries might look to people below, people on the banks, people on the ships—perfect, maybe, from far away. The light-polluted clouds hung purple and red against the fuzzy orange sky, and somebody's cell phone rang somewhere out by the water. A lonesome sound.

If she were really the girl in a book, then this would be the climax. But she was not naïve; she knew she was not the girl in a book.

He offered her money for a cab, but she said she'd walk. He said he'd limp. And then he kissed her. He kissed her face; he did not kiss her lips. He said her name. He put his hand against her ribs, then appeared to think better of it. He pinched her side and that was that. She said good-bye and started walking. She felt him watching, but she did not turn around. She was Lot's Wife in reverse. She was Orpheus, but with discipline. She walked all the way to Union Station without looking back.

◁▷

Her friend Mary Beth says that the sexiest—and saddest— words around are "It's my last night in town."

◁▷

Later that week, he left a note in her mailbox: TTM and his initials on a pale yellow Post-It. Her favorite abbreviation: Talk To Me.

She went into his office. He was on the phone, so she made herself busy by looking around at handsomely framed photos she'd looked at dozens of times before: her boss with friends, her boss with family, her boss shaking hands with other important bosses and men. He kept one particular photo on his low, glass-fronted bookcase, himself long ago, in Italy, with long hair and a beard, surrounded by other long-haired bearded men and beautiful women drinking wine on a train. He was even younger than her in that photo.

The sun shone in through Mies van der Rohe's high windows, and the light caught her engagement ring, turning it into a prism.

He hung up the phone and said her name. "I wanted to tell you that tomorrow is probably the last day I'll see you for a while."

"What?" she said. She had another week left to work before she moved away.

"I have to go on a trip the day after tomorrow. So this is it, babe."

"But that sucks," she said.

"I know, doesn't it just? But I wanted to tell you a story."

"Okay."

"So I'm always trying to figure out why the hell we do the work we do," he began, "and I came across this story in this book on archaeology. These archaeologists in Africa were working on research on hominids. They found this skeleton of a woman, a *homo erectus*, and it was 1.7 million years old—1.7 *million*. Her bones were completely pathological, deteriorated from a horrible disease. They did research and X-rays and figured out it was from a rare ailment called hypervitaminosis A—an excess of Vitamin A caused by eating too much meat. It still shows up rarely today in people like Eskimos who eat a lot of liver and things. The disease was in its most advanced stage. In fact, they discovered, this woman had actually died from it. And this was a remarkable thing—a remarkable thing."

"Why? Didn't people die pretty much all the time back then in horrible ways?"

"Yes, but this was a debilitating disease, one that would have made her immobile. Too weak to stand up, to walk, let alone hunt for food or water to drink. By rights, she should have died much earlier on, of starvation or exposure or predation from animals. But the fact that she died of her illness is what's so amazing. She lived on that long because someone else was taking care of her. Someone else was bothering—very likely against self-interest and at some considerable degree of personal risk—to provide her with shelter and food. Someone was sitting up with her through the long, dark African nights to scare away jackals and lions. And this person was doing it for no other reason than because he cared for her. This is one of the earliest instances of humans behaving with what I guess you'd call *humanity*. I suppose I like that story because it's about the origin of love, really. Why we decide we can and should help someone not because we'll get something out of it, but because that's just basic fucking decency."

"I like that story," she said. "But I need to go now, or I think I might cry."

"I know," he said. "I don't want to prolong this. Go on—leave early. Get out of here."

◄►

"Just because I think there's someone for everyone," said her old friend Mary Beth, "doesn't mean I think that there's only one someone."

◄►

She wasn't heading directly back to the suburbs that night, but was going instead to have dinner with her sister and friends. Riding the El to the north side, she did her best to be happy, though she felt beside herself, like her disappointment had taken the shape of a conjoined twin, occupying the blue velour and plastic seat beside her. The train was full, but no one else sat there.

Goddammit, don't cry, she told herself. She had a lot to be grateful for. He had helped her, given her a job, a really good summer, and hadn't that been just exactly what she'd asked for? What kind of idiot cried over getting what she'd asked for?

◁▷

Of course there really were a fair number of reasons to be that sad. The prehistoric woman in the story had died and the female war hero would lose the election later that fall. There were, as always, all sorts of indications that the world was a difficult and a disappointing place.

But within these signs were other signs that there was a lot to be said for trying and failing, trying for trying's sake; indications that within the inevitability of disappointment and frustration lies the perverse pleasure of wanting something very badly and still not getting it, of carrying on in spite—or maybe because—of the way that we can and should do our best to save each other, even though it is futile to expect that any one other person can truly save us.

◁▷

Her last day of working with him was an anti-climax. That night, a Wednesday, was their regularly scheduled softball game, and she and some of the interns went to watch him and the more athletic members of the staff play on the fields just blocks from the water. His ankle was still in poor shape, and watching him she tried hard to ignore how old he looked. How they'd all deteriorate and die no matter how much anyone else cared for them.

They lost.

After the game, she and her boss sat straddling the rough-grained bench, facing each other—behind him the ships anchored for the night on the lake, and behind her the skyline and the interns whose names he still couldn't keep straight. The sun was going down. The lights were coming on. He wore a silver saint medal on a chain around his neck, a baseball cap, and his gap-toothed smile. In his rough smoker's voice he said, "Well, Kathleen. This is it. Good-bye. If you ever want to come back, we could do it differently next time. You've got gifts, and we should use them."

She nodded, at a loss for anything more to say. She hugged him and got up to leave. "Kathleen," he said, as she began to walk away. "Kathleen, Kathleen, I hope you'll come back."

◄►

When she and her husband are driving away, way out west where reception is poor, where shadows stretch mountain-shaped and swarthy over hollows and valleys, she thinks of him and their recent proximity. How all that summer was like coming close to a city she'd love nothing more than to live in, but having to drive by.

You can get the radio stations to tune in high and clear, but you can't quite get there. Not from here.

I WILL
CATCH
YOU

I WRITE FOR AN online magazine whose motto is this: "We're the people your students are plagiarizing."

I'm also a teacher. Three times this semester, I have been plagiarized upon. You will notice that I didn't say "three times *that I know of.*"

At the start of each semester, both I and my syllabi tell my students this:

> Plagiarism is the use of the words and/or ideas of another as if they were one's own and without acknowledgment of their source. In other words, plagiarism is stealing another person's words without crediting them or using proper citation. Sometimes, plagiarism is unintentional. If this happens, we'll sit down and look at your work. If you plagiarize intentionally, you will fail this course. Be warned that such a record remains in a student's permanent file, and can also result in probation or expulsion.

This is in the boilerplate.

Because boilerplate can be boring, I tell them also: "The Internet has made it incredibly easy to cheat, but so too has it made cheating incredibly easy to catch."

Many of them apparently choose not to listen, or perhaps to listen only to the first half. But my job here in the academy is not to teach listening comprehension. Not exactly.

◀▶

If you are a cheater, I will not know it right away. I will not sense it based on the way you sit in my class, the way you raise or do not raise your hand. I will not be able to apprehend that you are too lazy or too ignorant or too careless or too indifferent to do your own work based on any physical or behavioral characteristics. If anything, you will look like a fine, upstanding young man—blue jeans and T-shirts and even a wedding ring, but no cap slung low over your bright blue eyes, no hoodie over your downy brown hair, no resting your chin on the desk like you can't wait to haul yourself off somewhere else.

But when you turn in a response paper to Susan Sontag's *Regarding the Pain of Others* that contains a paragraph that begins: "Her new book is a profound rethinking of the intersection of 'news,' art, and understanding in the contemporary depiction of war and disaster," a paragraph lifted word-for-word from the book's dust jacket, I will know you are a cheater.

I will contact you and politely tell you that I know, and you will email back, "I did not plagiarize the Sontag paper I just listed the ideas from the book that she presented in her book. She mentioned all those places in her book so I just reiterated them in my paper."

Because I believe that two-way communication is crucial to the educational process, we will discuss why this is neither a valid excuse, nor a valid practice. And because I believe in learning opportunities and teachable moments, I will give you the benefit of the doubt, and you will tell me, "I will try to work as hard as I can to prove that that is not who I am." I may conjecture in my heart that this *is* who you are, but I will forgive you this time, because I believe in second chances and because I want all my students to have a reasonable grasp at success. But from that point on I will keep my eye on you and everyone else in the class even more than before.

◂▸

In another of my classes—the only one of the three I'm teaching this semester in which I've yet to catch a cheater—we are reading Greek philosophers on the Good. The Beautiful. The benefits of Virtue. But I know, I know—this small regional university isn't the Symposium. We're not all going to go walking with Socrates. We're not all going to compose edifying dialogues or didactic epistles.

Plato says: "There is poetry, which, as you know, is complex and manifold. All creation or passage of non-being into being is poetry or making, and the processes of all art are creative; and the masters of arts are all poets or makers."

I know that you will not all be poets, and you will not all be makers, and that many of you think it is a waste of time to think and to create.

Some of you will not want, as one term-paper-mill website puts it, to spend "hours in a library or online searching for a paper on your topic—only to end up with no paper and no quality information . . . only to get a garbage grade."

You will feel this way because you believe that the answer to this paper mill's question, "Do you have better things to do with your time than spend it writing a useless paper?" is yes.

And I pity you. And I do my best to move you to feel otherwise. But sometimes I can't move you. In this case, I will make you learn anyway, in spite of yourself, and in spite of your bad attitude, and if you won't, I will punish you.

◁▷

Plato also says—and this is a big quote, because it's an elegant idea, but it's not mine, and I need to give credit:

> And the same holds true of love. For you may say generally that all desire of good and happiness is only the great and subtle power of love; but they who are drawn towards him by any other path, whether the path of money-making or gymnastics or philosophy, are not called lovers—the name of the whole is appropriated to those whose affection takes one form only—they alone are said to love, or to be lovers.

Although it is my heartfelt desire for you to all be seekers, lovers, I know that you do not all love learning for learning's sake. I'm curiously okay with that.

The ideal circumstance for the academy would be that everyone has come here simply for his or her love of learning, but frankly that is unrealistic. Some of you are here for that reason, but others of you are here because of hegemony—a word I try to teach you—because this is the logical next middle-class step after high school; because of a desire to make more money, to garner more professional respect.

Though I want you to love what we do at this small religious university, I know that sometimes you won't.

So the revised ideal is to create an environment in which learning can—really *has to*—occur. It's not always very pretty, but sometimes this ideal is achieved by simply making learning the easiest thing that can happen.

Isn't it easiest for everybody that you just learn about this stuff and write about it in a manner that is smart and a manner that is yours?

How can I make that easier than by allowing you to plagiarize your paper?

By really kicking your ass if you plagiarize your paper. You will fail my class. You will get kicked out of school.

◀▶

You might think *She won't catch me*, but there you are wrong. I will catch you. I will catch you. I will catch you. I will catch you.

◀▶

You can't turn in a paragraph like this:

In this sad, cool, short novel, Duras tells the largely autobiographical story of a 15-year-old European girl's first affair with an older Chinese man in French Indochina during the 1930s. Stereotypes and expectations are inverted: she is poor, he wealthy; she seduces him, not vice versa; she controls the relationship, does not love him though he is hopelessly smitten with her, and she dictates all the terms, including how and when it ends. Duras uses cinematic techniques—flashbacks and forwards, repetitions, incidents cut up and interrupted by seemingly unrelated descriptions—and switches between first and third person to enrich what at first seems a fairly dry and unadorned narrative. A depressing yet eloquent work of art.

and—just because you changed the original "besotted" to "smitten"—expect me not to suspect it comes from here: http://allreaders.com/topics/Info_1908.asp.

The average college student does not describe narratives as "dry" or "unadorned." The ambitious plagiarizer must dig deeper.

You can't turn in a paragraph in which you observe nonchalantly of the classic *Dispatches* that "Herr's field of vision is broad but always at its center are the 'grunts,' the infantrymen who invariably carried themselves through the war with dignity and a carefully cultivated and life-sustaining combination of humor and cynicism," and expect me not to suspect you've paid a visit to the Houghton Mifflin textbook site for the *Heath Anthology of American Literature* (fifth edition).

The average college student does not describe authorial vision as "broad." The ambitious plagiarizer must go further.

◆▷

My friend Chris Hutson, also a professor, remarked of you, my first and most egregious cheater this semester, my blue-eyed innocent: "Tell Mr. Plagiarist to eat a bowl of fuck."

It crossed my mind to tell you this, oh yes it did, but I am a fair instructor, always in search of an opportunity for learning. I want to be sure you understand why plagiarizing is wrong, why you will get in trouble if you do it.

But if you refuse to own that fact, refuse to admit that plagiarizing is a morally bankrupt act, an act which hurts you, the person whose words you stole, and everyone else in the class who does his or her own work, an act which should be loathsome to you entirely in and of itself, then I will force you to own this fact in another, more brutal and less abstract way.

The reason you should not plagiarize is the same reason you should not rob a bank: you might get caught. And if you get caught, the consequences are really bad. Should they be really bad? Yes. I don't think anyone with a belief in the value of honesty and ethical behavior can dispute that.

◆

There are many features of my job as a professor that I find enriching, fulfilling. One feature that does not thrill me is that it's my job to terrify you, hopefully enough to keep you from cheating, but otherwise to terrify you of ever doing it again.

It would be nice if I could inspire you not to cheat—to want to do right simply because doing right is a good and pure thing. And I do inspire some of you, lead you to love. But failing that, there's always fear.

No society has been able ever to function without some kind of punishment. Some kind of threat. The academy's not so different from the rest of society.

Niccolò Machiavelli, another author I like to look at with my classes, asks in *The Prince*: "whether it be better to be loved than feared or feared than loved?" (*The Prince* may have been satire, or may have been serious, but that's not the issue here; the issue is that I'm citing it properly.)

He answers his own question: "that one should wish to be both, but, because it is difficult to unite them in one person, it is much safer to be feared than loved, when, of the two, either must be dispensed with."

Why choose fear over love?

"Because this is to be asserted in general of men, that they are ungrateful, fickle, false, cowardly, covetous," and because "men have less scruple in offending one who is belovéd than one who is feared, for love is preserved by the link of obligation which, owing to the baseness of men, is broken at every opportunity for their advantage; but fear preserves you by a dread of punishment which never fails.

◀▶

Please don't fuck with me; I'm not to be fucked with.

◀▶

When I was younger, I wanted all my students to really like me; to want to be my friend. Now, if they want that, that's fine, but all I really strive to be is tough but fair.

Hence the boilerplate. Hence "you will fail this course."

Still, I think I'm actually a lot more lovable than fearsome. When I walk into a room, I still look so small, so young, that you say things like, "You're the teacher? No way," to which I reply, "Way." But your not knowing to be afraid will make you more afraid when you force me to crack down.

◄►

You can't turn in a paper that says that, in her poem "It Feels a Shame to be Alive," "Emily Dickinson reflects on the loss of lives during subsequent battles, and because of Dickinson's use of intangible and universal language, we can read the same poem in the context of any war in history and apply it to all of the Americans that have lost their lives to ensure our freedom," and just because you used the Microsoft Word thesaurus feature to change "abstract" to "intangible" expect me not to suspect that you ripped the entire thing off a website featuring an explication of the same poem by somebody named Cindy McCutcheon from goddamn Georgetown.

The average college student—especially one now notorious to me as the perpetrator of the boneheaded fourth-grade-book-report move of using the jacket copy from a book as his own original paragraph—does not refer to language as "intangible" and "universal."

The ambitious plagiarizer needs to press beyond the first Google hit that comes up when he types the name of the poem he is supposed to analyze for his midterm.

◄►

I will be sitting in a coffee shop grading when I start to read "your" paper. There will of course be free wireless, so I will use my laptop to uncover your deceit with dizzying speed. I will feel sick to my stomach. I will find the number of the registrar's office online, call them, tell them what I found. They will put an F after your name and a hold on your record so you can't drop the class; can't take the easy way out. Next I will email you: "I'm very disappointed to have to write to you about this," I will begin, and this will be true. "But you need to know," I'll continue, and I'll explain all that will happen to you: "You will fail this course with no chance to withdraw, and the record of your academic dishonesty will go in your student disciplinary file. I am very sorry to have to do this, but plagiarism is a major offense, and cannot be permitted."

◄►

It will get ugly. It will get sad. As my friend Elisa puts it, "Kids when caught: quite a phenomenon."

You will email me thrice on that first night, and you will be implausible and defensive and loose with your grammar: "For the mid-term I research this poem a lot. I read several different views of the poem. If it seems to look like the paper you suggest I might of just memorized so thoughts from there and used those points and did not realize I was doing that."

You will be presumptuous: "If this is your final decision than that is fine, but please give me another chance. You can fail me on the mid-term but please do not fail me in the class. I did not do that on purpose. Please rethink your decision. If your mind will not change and you can not give me a second chance, well than have a good life and I hope everything works out for you."

You will be conciliatory, desperate, and outright delusional: "Also if that is not enough I am willing to write as many papers as you want or do whatever you want to make this up. Please."

You will go so far as to email me files of both your plagiarized paper and that of young Cindy McCutcheon, with the cryptic, misspelled denial: "I found that poem you talked about and I do not see any resenblance."

But I will see the resemblance. And I will stick by my decision.

◀▶

You will ambush me the next morning outside my office, before my 8:00 A.M. class, tears in your eyes, doughy face wet with rain, proffering a new paper, still plagiarized, and a wild story but not an apology.

You will cry and you will beg and I will show no mercy. No mercy. Your eyes will get wider and wetter and bluer than the sky and I will not back down because you are a cheater. You will tell me you regret what you did—*my wife*, you'll say; *my son*—but I will not care because you are the one who betrayed them. You are the one.

You will not be able to believe this is happening. You will not be able to accept what you've done. You will demand an appeal, so the university will have to schedule an Academic Dishonesty Hearing Panel before which you will appear to plead your weak case.

You will write me email after late-night email in the ensuing days, typing sentences like "Getting an education so I can support my son is what I treasure the most. I would never do that to disgrace myself to him," but the problem will be that you did. You did.

◀▶

In the plodding days leading up to your hearing, you will persist in attending class—which I will admit is your right, until a final decision is made—as though nothing is wrong. Meanwhile, you will leave in my mailbox another plagiarized paper with the handwritten scrawl, "I know this does not change anything so you can rip this up, throw it away, shred it, spit on it, or put a curse on it so I have bad luck and die, whatever. I just wanted to turn in a paper that you do not think I plagerized, so that's why I wrote this. Thanks."

It will have a p.s that reads, "I wasn't referring to anything in the above comments, just me being stupid as normal."

I will be vaguely freaked out, but mostly annoyed. I will keep insisting that you get what you deserve. You will keep coming to class. You will compliment my outfits, tell me where I've set the dry-erase marker when I misplace it. You will laugh with your classmates and act like we're pals. I will hate having to look at you. We are not friends; I am your teacher.

◄►

Outside the hearing room, you will be dressed in your best button-down shirt and tie like a scrubbed-up defendant on CourtTV. Your pale blue shirt will bring out your bright blue eyes. Your friends will walk by and joke with you that you've never looked better, that you clean up real nice, and you will laugh back nervously, but not so nervously that they'd notice, and you will agree.

And they will say, "What's up, Mikey? You got an interview or something?"

And you will look them in the eye, and cast an eye over at me, and you will lie again. "Yes," you will say. "That's what it is. An interview."

And they will slap you on the back and smile and start to walk away, "Good luck, man. Good luck."

But your luck has run out, and you will be found guilty.

There will be a tape recorder, three panel members including two professors and one student, plus an outside observer. There will be me, and you, and your support person—another professor, there to provide moral support. The proceedings will be tedious, but in the end, they'll decide rightly. They'll find in my favor.

You will fail the paper, fail the course, and have a big black CHEATER mark on your permanent record, and you might not get into dental school, and your life might be ruined. This will not be something I wanted. No, I let you transfer into the class off the waitlist, and I believed you when you emailed me early in the semester, "I really enjoy your class and I am glad I was able to transfer in to it."

I edited and proofread your personal statement for dental school not once but twice. I gave you a second chance. But now you have to pay. And I am sad too, but life is sometimes sad, even when it's fair.

◄►

After everything is over—after your hearing, and the catching and giving of second chances to two subsequent, lesser cheaters— I will go out with a colleague and drink Manhattans. One per plagiarizer. I will get very drunk, and end up hungover.

I will think back on what's happened, and how isn't it funny that the first religiously affiliated school I've taught at has turned out to be the cheatingest. Maybe that means something, and maybe it doesn't. I will wonder how many plagiarizers I'll catch during my whole year here; how many my colleagues will catch; have already caught. I will decide the answer is a lot.

◄►

In the end, maybe I can't catch everyone. Maybe some of you will be able to get away with it. But it is my job to make it so hard for you to do so that you will wind up wishing you had just written the fucking paper.

Even if you do cheat and manage to pull it off successfully (i.e., not get caught) you will probably accidentally learn something in the process, in which case I—and all that is honest and right in this world—still win. But that doesn't mean you lose. You win too, because the goal of this game is that you end up learning.

I am not a downer, and I am not a cynic. There are students in all of my classes who are there because they genuinely love to learn. My job is to make sure you, the cheater, get a shittier grade than those students.

I suppose that here, one could say that Foucault wins again—that under these circumstances, the function of education is effectively reduced to cops and robbers. And though I do not like when this happens—do not enjoy when a job that I love, by necessity involves my playing a disciplinarian role that I hate—sometimes I must be a cop. It's not pretty, but there you have it: the possibility of the exertion of brute force is not the essence of the higher educational system, but it's one of the preconditions for it.

◆▸

So don't give me your stolen, copied, borrowed, bought, or bribed essays, and don't feel like you have to be perfect when you hand in your work. Give me your tense shifts, your misspellings, and your passive verbs. Your "on cores" for "encores" and your "thens" for "thans." Your "ados" instead of "adieus." Your plurals instead of your possessives. But please, please, please don't give me Cindy McCutcheon's paper from goddamn Georgetown. Come on people. Take some responsibility. Be good students; be good citizens.

Give me your papers you've written because you've loved them. Give me your papers like the one I got a week after all the cheating dust settled, the paper where you say:

> Is this good writing? I would say that it is, but what do I know. I am finally finishing my first writing class, I have

dropped out of two classes prior to now. So what I think really doesn't matter that much now does it. I am not rich or dating anyone of any importance. I despise George Bush and Capitalism. I think gay people should be allowed to be married and that Marijuana should be legal. Who am I to say that anything is good or bad? I am utterly insignificant. However there is one significant detail that I am overlooking. This paper that I have set out to write is my paper. I am writing it for you but it isn't yours, it is mine. These words and thoughts are mine. That is what makes the first paragraph beautiful and good.

I will get papers like these from lots of students, and they will not be perfect, and they will have problems. But they will be in your words, your very own words, and you are all my students and I am your teacher and we will all be learning. Honestly, we will.

STAIRCASE

i was sitting in mcsorley's. outside it was New York and beautifully snowing.

—e. e. cummings

cSORLEY'S OLD ALE House is the oldest Irish pub in New York City. What kind of old? They claim they opened in 1854. What kinds of ale? Two: light and dark.

e. e. cummings calls McSorley's "snugandevil." That was 1923. Almost eighty-five years later—January 2007—it is still both of those things. e. e. cummings says it twice: "Inside snugandevil."

McSorley's is in the East Village. You walk in with your friends, and they seat you with strangers. Snug and evil. Fun and scary. Sawdust floors and newsprint walls, of which cummings says, "the slobbering walls filthily push witless creases of scream-ing warmth chuck pillows are noise funnily swallows swallowing revolvingly pompous."

When we are there—Elise, Beth, and me—it is raining, not snowing: wet and disappointing, a slobbery kiss. This is because the planet is visibly warming. We can't help remarking: Al Gore must disapprove.

Elise lives in Brooklyn, Beth in Chicago, I in Tacoma. The Chicago Bears have just defeated the Seattle Seahawks, but nobody cares, because we are on the East Coast. The New England Patriots have just beaten the San Diego Chargers, and everyone in the bar is waving their arms and cheering at the TV, but mostly we don't want to talk about sports.

McSorley's was one of the last men-only taverns in the city. Its most famous slogans today are "Be Good or Be Gone" and "We were here before *you* were born." Prior to 1970, they used a third slogan, "Good Ale, Raw Onions, and No Ladies." Women were not permitted until then, just ten short years before my birth—when the National Organization for Women sued McSorley's and won.

Some men who drank here before I was born? Boss Tweed, Abraham Lincoln, Teddy Roosevelt, and Woody Guthrie. LeRoi Jones before he changed his name to Amiri Baraka, Brendan Behan, and Paul Blackburn.

Two men who are drinking here with us on this lukewarm night before Martin Luther King Jr. Day? Daniel and Steven—Dan and Steve—to whose rough-hewn round table Elise and Beth and I have been boisterously ushered by the Irish barkeep, trying to keep as many patrons seated in the space as possible. Originally, we had seated ourselves separately, but another large party came in, so we got bumped and were told, "Make friends!" If I were to use French to describe the evening, the theme would be *l'esprit d'escalier*, the wit of the staircase, a handy term coined by Diderot the Encyclopedist: the frustration of thinking of precisely the right comeback, only much too late.

At first, this is so much fun! I am good at finding funny stuff to say, moving my bright red lips, speaking interesting things. Steve and Dan both live in Manhattan. They are in their early thirties. They have been best friends since their crazy college days. Steve—swarthy, dark eyed, with slick black hair—works in the tech support department for some boring and prosperous company. Dan—chiseled jaw, dimpled chin, blond faux-hawk, and blue eyes—is a financial analyst. He works in the financial district. We nod. We see.

Beth and I are sisters with a lot of free time at this time of year—she is a freelance photographer, and I am a college professor—so we are visiting Elise, an artist, who lives in an illegal squat in Greenpoint. Elise works in the packing-and-shipping department at Christie's.

"We got a bubble-wrap professional in our midst," quips Steve.

Elise smiles, shrugs her shoulders inside her purple thrift-store sweatshirt.

Steve is awaiting the arrival of his girlfriend. Both Dan and Steve are waiting on a call from their good friend Donkey. After that they will all go to dinner somewhere. They invite us, but we politely decline. We have other plans.

Introductions dispensed with, we all shake hands, and then Steve says to me, "Dan and I would like to invite you to join our boy band."

"Oh?" I say, then notice that we three are all wearing some variation on the theme of blue jeans and short-sleeved brown shirts over long-sleeved white tops. "You got the memo about the boy-band color scheme, I see," I say. We laugh. How innovative to ask a girl to join your boy band.

Beth has brought her digital camera—her Nikon, the good one—pictures from the day, our stay in NYC so far, still loaded inside.

"Take a picture of our band!" says Dan, and Beth obliges. She insured her camera last fall, in part for peace of mind under just such circumstances. She places the costly piece of equipment into Dan's outstretched hands so he can see the result. The picture is great.

"Hey, you're really good," Dan says, scanning through the photos, and it's true. She is. "Now take one of just me."

She does. I appraise it.

"You should have her do it again," I tell him, in my faux-wise voice. "And try to do it with only the left ear showing this time."

"What's wrong with my ears?" he asks.

"It's not just your ears—it's everyone's. It's a portrait photographer trick. People just look more attractive that way."

He obeys.

The head bartender at McSorley's has wide ears, a broad face, and a huge smile that never seems to reach his eyes. He claims in a brogue that he can carry twenty-two half-pint glasses at a time in one ham-fisted hand. He keeps bringing us more and more, darks and lights, and why fight it, we figure. We completely believe him. We decide to try it. We practice with our empties. With her long, pale, artistic fingers, dexterous Elise can do eleven. I can only do nine. Dan's hands are much bigger. He lifts nineteen. Steve is building an ill-advised half-pint pyramid. Dan's hands—square with close-cut fingernails—keep moving from the glasses to my thigh. "Snugandevil."

The time blurs by. An American flag hangs behind us. There is a war on, boys. The Irish-American Americana on the walls in mismatched dark frames has never been dusted. Memorabilia and nostalgia. We will none of us ever be this young again.

Another of our friends arrives: tall Jack Huffman in his gray-and-black striped scarf. The barkeep lumbers by and moves us again, to the end of a half-occupied rectangular slab of a table.

I try to maneuver out of Dan's way, but he sticks close by my side. Beth is rolling her eyes. "Why don't you say something?" she says.

"I will if I have to," I tell her. But it seems so silly. So déclassé. So abrupt to have to interject and say, "Hey, quit breaking the social contract like that. Hey, I shouldn't have to say this, but your idea of a good time is ruining mine."

A double-entendre graces the T-shirt of the guy now seated across from us, a picture of Cheney, above which is emblazoned, "My Dick Would Make a Better Vice President."

Dan and I discuss the ramifications of this. Does this guy mean his actual unit would make a better vice president? Or does he just know a guy named Dick who would be less of a fascist maniac?

"Hey, Kathy-Kathleen," says Dan, redoubling his efforts now that Steve's perky, blonde girlfriend has arrived. Poor horny Dan is so sad and lonely. "Give me your number?"

"Okay, ready?" I say, "It's nine-one-one."

"Seriously, give it to me," he says, pressing his face close to mine.

"No way," I say. "It's mine." I tell him I'm married.

"Okay, fine. Then I'll give you mine," he says, grabbing my phone off the table and typing in his number.

McSorley's has a kitchen, but it appears that the only food they serve is the stinky cheese platter referenced by their misogynistic old sign, the ostensibly manly hors d'oeuvres that come on a stark white plate piled with white cheese, a plastic-wrapped white pack of white saltines, and mounds and piles of sliced white onions.

Elise looks up from the bit she had been adventurously trying with our other new stranger-friends at her end of the table and sighs a sigh of sympathy for me. She cannot believe this guy.

"Hey, Dan," she says. "Wanna try one of these?"

Drunk, Dan is hungry. But I want to mess with him. "You'll smell so bad if you do," I tell him. "What if you end up needing to make out with someone later?"

He declines.

A familiar song comes over the speakers. Justin Timberlake in a high falsetto: "Dirty babe . . ."

"Do you like J-Tim?" asks Dan.

"Yeah, sure—"

"Cuz you got a sexy back!" he says, hand sliding up and down it, making his way under both the brown and white shirts.

"Jesus *Christ*," says Beth.

"Dan, seriously," I say, cringing and pulling away. "I'm so not interested. Knock it off."

At this point, we want to leave, but we are waiting for our other friends, real friends, friends I haven't seen in years. They are on their way, and they are almost here, so we stay.

Jeremy and Jessica finally show up. We order another round and toast their arrival.

"You have to look someone in the eye when you cheers, or else it's seven years' bad sex," Dan says, banging his half-pint glass of dark so hard into mine that light splashes out.

"That's news I can use." I smile, like the bartender, not using my eyes.

"So now, when we're having sex later tonight, it'll be awesome." Grins. Big white teeth.

"So where did you guys go to school anyway?" I ask.

"George Washington University," they reply in unison, assholes in stereo, and it all makes sense.

"I went to GW," I say.

"No way! Didn't you just love it?" says Steve.

"Didn't you have the best time?" says Dan.

"Oh yeah," I lie. I loved my time in college, but it was a complicated love—was it the politics? the climate? the conspicuous imbalance between people with wealth and people without it? Unavoidable at GW in particular and in D.C. in general were brash, pushy men like these; men with huge senses of entitlement, roving hands, no apparent worries, and no apparent manners. I like my memories, but I haven't been back to the place since graduation.

"Hail to the buff! Hail to the blue! Hail to the buff and blue!" they cry, launching into the GW fight song. "All our lives we'll be proud to say we hail from Gee Double-U!"

Jeremy looks across the table at me, eyebrows raised high. I shrug. Sigh. Make a finish-your-drink-and-we'll-get-out-of-here gesture.

Turns out that Dan and Steve—both of whom graduated before I even got to D.C.—were in a fraternity. They lived in the
same red brick frat house where a close friend of mine was date-
raped by one of the brothers; the same frat house where lots of
girls likely met the same fate; the same frat house with an enormous branching shoe tree outside, pairs of footwear hung over
the scraggly limbs, shoes tossed by various brothers in order to
commemorate each girl they had banged.

In his poem "I was sitting in McSorley's," cummings writes
of arriving at an "instant of semiluminous nausea," and at this
point, I feel there has to be something I can say. It is getting too ridiculous, embarrassing. I am twenty-six. A grown woman. A professor and an editor, and Dan will not cut it out with the hands on
my hands, the hands on my thighs. He will not keep away.

And I hate that he is stronger than me. That he is more powerful and richer and a way bigger dick than I will ever be and that
none of this matters to his quality of life, and that he will always
be this way and will always get away with it.

He is huge. I am gamine. He is nouveau riche; I am at best
rather *pauvre*. He is an absolute goober and a crap conversationalist, and I like witty aperçus; I like to accrue them. But
sometimes the rate of speed with which I do so, obviously, is
inadequate for the situation at hand. That is part of why I am a
writer, maybe.

Sometimes, after I have been mad and unable to think of anything to say, I have that *esprit d'escalier*: "_____," I say. I say
nothing. I am the empty set.

I am good at being witty when everything is fine. When I am
trying to be winsome. When things are going okay. And I am

smart. And I am charming. Enchanting! I can make everyone feel so very *enchanté*.

But this guy. This guy! This dude in the bar, this frat-boy rapist from GW who keeps touching me. Trying to kiss me. Asking me questions and not even pretending to care about the answers. Disgusted—as much with my dumbstruck self as with him—I get up to pee, to escape.

Beth, in my absence, gets all up in Dan's stupid, beefy, handsome face and says, "Not everyone in this bar wants to be touched by you, so stop being an asshole. And if you touch my sister again I'll kick you in the fucking balls."

Beth has never been one to suffer from *l'esprit d'escalier*—she says what she needs to say at the party, before the stairs.

She is the girl who, when she tells a story, will be interrupted inevitably by somebody saying, "No way, oh my God, you *didn't* say that. Did you?" And she will reply, "The fuck I didn't," or if she needs to be polite, "Oh, yes I did." Me, not so much.

When I come back from the bathroom I sit down again, but far away from Dan. And he doesn't try to touch me. And he and Steve and the girlfriend get up to leave. And he pays for all our drinks.

Elise tries to pay for hers, tries to give him some cash, because she is an independent woman and a total class act, but Beth and I wave her fistful of bills away.

"No way, Elise, don't pay. You don't need to. He doesn't need it. He doesn't deserve it."

And we are all able to sit at our own nice round table, with only our real friends, and enjoy the rest of our time at "snugand-evil" McSorley's.

The spirit of the staircase. I suppose for *l'esprit d'escalier* to be truly the subject of this essay, I would have to tell you now, right here, since I have had so much time to perfect it, the comeback to Dan I thought of later that night, the one that caused me to sit bolt upright on the air mattress in Elise's illegal loft, where I slept fitfully next to Beth. Or maybe the comeback that I thought of on the plane back to SeaTac. Or the one I came up with at home at my own kitchen table, recounting the night to my husband. But I haven't thought of anything especially witty, except lines in the vein of "Stop touching me, dickface," or others of that ilk. What can I say? The situation didn't call for subtlety.

And anyway, my best bons mots are, to my alternate delight and chagrin, chiefly in the service of charm, chiefly in the service of—were I to be reductive—what one might call the feminine. Even when I am being witty and "mean" with my friends, making fun of other people, it stems from my desire to amuse, to please, to make sure people like me.

A friend and colleague of mine, a PhD in religion and all-around smart guy, once said to me at a party, "Wit is the bridge from lens to bitch." I didn't know what he meant at the time, but I liked it so much, I stuck it in my notebook. But now I think I see. Wit and comedy are all well and good in men—accepted, expected—but in women, it can be more dicey. You can go from being a fun-time happy party girl, all nicey nice, to total bitch in under ten seconds. And it sucks to think you might have to. It is all too often necessary to go ahead and be a so-called bitch just for the sake of having a voice.

But I like manners, and I like politeness. I like respect and hate to think that I should have to fight for it. But sometimes a woman has to fight, and simply expecting things doesn't get them.

So in a sense I can't do things my way. Not totally. Can't say what I want to, can't leave unsaid what I don't want to say.

So, what should I have said to Dan? What should I say to people like him to be all bitchy-polite and in the moment, without waiting for the regret, for *l'esprit d'escalier*?

Get off my fucking staircase, please. Please, don't touch me, and get out of my way.

TO BUILD
A QUIET CITY
IN MY MIND

Your absence breeds / A longer silence through the rooms. We haunt ourselves.

—WELDON KEES, "RETURN OF THE GHOST"

I AM IN LOVE with another man, but my husband doesn't mind.

I have come to the city to find this man's apartments. Over the course of the week, I will seek out all nine—one in Brooklyn, eight in Manhattan—but I will never find the man himself.

I am in love with a dead man.

I love his poems, his writings, his looks, his life, and the way the Library of Congress Cataloging-in-Publication Data at the front of his handful of books reads: "Kees, Weldon, 1914–1955?"

I am in love with Weldon Kees: poet, painter, and jazz musician. Creator of Robinson. Mysterious suicide.

Or I am in love with Weldon Kees—photographer, filmmaker, and cultural critic—creator of Robinson and mysterious disappearee.

This morning, I wake up with an aching head and a fading black stamp inked on the back of my right hand that says DEAD. It haunts my skin like a ghost. It faces away, toward my fingers, upside down to me, but upright to others.

Last night, Beth and I, along with Elise and a bunch of our friends who live in the city had gone to a bar in Brooklyn. The black-clad man checking IDs at the door stamped our hands with the word "dead" to signify we were of age to drink. "Enjoy the afterlife," he said as we slipped through the black velvet curtains, beneath a box fan facing out the transom, blowing silver mylar streamers like rainclouds.

Today, as wet gray light slides through the blinds on the windows of Elise's illegal loft where Beth and I are lying atop an air mattress, I know I am alive and will feel even more so after a shower and some coffee. My dead-yet-not-dead status makes me think of the disappearance of Weldon Kees, how he is one or the other, obviously—either you're dead or you're not—but he is not clearly either, or at least he wasn't for a long time.

He had been talking for years about committing suicide or starting over in Mexico when he vanished. That was almost fifty-two years ago, in San Francisco, July 1955.

My sister Beth and I have both come to New York in January 2007 for a visit, her to meet with photo editors at agencies and magazines, me for Kees and a launch party in Boston at the end of the week. But first and foremost we've come to feel more alive.

Weldon Kees makes me feel more alive every time I read him—every time I read his biography, even. He makes me write "yes, yes, yes" in the margins of his poems, at the ends of his letters. I feel like I get him so well, that he would surely get me—that is, if circumstances had been such that he ever could have met me. His wife called him Weld, but I've decided that I'd have called him Kees, as though we were working toward the same goals for some fabulous team.

Beth and I are in the middle of a long, slow season. I am a college professor and my university is on J-term, which means I still get paid, but I don't have to teach, leaving me nothing but time to kill in Tacoma, Washington. Beth is a freelance photographer. Her bread and butter is shooting for the business school of a Chicago university, but everyone's on winter holiday so there's no one to photograph.

We are both succeeding, but feeling success-less. We are feeling that maybe we are getting somewhere, but not fast enough, and whenever we arrive, "the room is cold, the words in the books are cold; / And the question of whether we get what we ask for / Is absurd." "What we have learned," we are finding "is not what we were / told." Delays and frustrations were bringing us down, so we decided to quit our bitching and take a break, and now here we are and already we are having the best time.

"Are you guys hungry?" Elise calls from the base of the stairs leading to our sleeping space. "Are you guys awake?"

Elise is from Ohio. She is talented and beautiful. Our sleeping space is set up behind a cloud of what look like handmade curtains, but which are actually part of her latest installation, a tribute to her dead grandmother—childhood and memory. The last time I saw her before this visit, she was rocking a femme-hawk, but she's grown it out. Now her dull brown hair is elegantly ratty, forming a shabby bird's nest of epic proportions.

"Starving," Beth answers.

"Great. I'll have Tom start breakfast."

Elise's boyfriend, Tom, is a dead ringer for the young Bob Dylan.

The two of them live with approximately eight other people in a commercial/industrial space they have illegally turned residential. Their flatmates include a transgendered New Zealander, a female drag queen, a composer with a deal on Nonesuch Records, a small-press editor, and a woman from France, who seems to wear only a red bathrobe for the duration of our visit, and who shuffles in and out of the kitchen gruffly, but never speaks. Every couple or set of roommates has their own loft, and shares the single kitchen and bathroom built into the center of the compound—like living in a hostel—but it has to be this way, or else they might get caught. All the rooms have heavy blinds to keep the light inside at night so they don't get found out and evicted.

The place used to be a mortuary with a coffin factory in the basement and a funeral parlor on the main floor, where they all live now. When they first moved in, they had to clean out jars and vials of sharp-smelling liquids, caustic cleansers, and embalming fluids. The basement beneath them has been taken over by welders, metal sculptors who like to work on their heavy projects late into the night. We can hear them clanging, sometimes, and imagine the heat below our feet.

When I peek out the curtain on my way to the shower, the streets are still slick with listless rain, just as they were when I arrived on my redeye yesterday. "Seattle weather: it has rained for weeks in this town." Elise says it's been this way for what feels like forever, an unseasonably warm winter, and I feel as though the Pacific Northwestern climate I was trying to escape has followed me.

Quick and wiry, Tom's an excellent cook. He and Elise feed Beth and me brunch—eggs and coffee, bananas and grapes, pears and pancakes—then they roll us a joint and we all four get high. Kees smoked up with Khalil Gibran Jr., a painter and the son of the poet, on the beach in Provincetown, a place I used to live. A place I miss. I picture this and smile after a deep inhale.

Tom, employed as a decorative painter during the week, decides to stay in and work on his own paintings, while Elise and Beth and I take the subway to visit the galleries in Chelsea: airy, brightly lit, warm and dry spaces in the middle of the dim and rainy Saturday.

Weldon Kees wrote often about interior spaces—room after room after room after room—though his rooms were typically austere and empty at best, severe and disquieting at worst. "The room was monstrous, overgrown," he writes in "First Anniversary." "Love," he writes, "is a sickroom with the roof half gone / Where nights go down in a continual rain." But if it's bad in the rooms, it's worse outside, where "The ragged trees in lightning, blacker than before, / Moved nearer to the room."

It is important to me to try to see these rooms, places where he invented his own still scenes, ghostly vignettes with the air sucked out. I want to see the places where he felt so trapped, where he lived when he wrote, "The crack is moving down the wall. / Defective plaster isn't all the cause. / We must remain until the roof falls in."

I want to see the places where he fought with his wife and received rejection letters, the places where he wrote, "Held in the rouged and marketable glow / Beyond Third Avenue, the city hums / Like muffled bees. / Sheeted, we lie / Above the streets, where headlights / Search the mirrors through the heat / And move on, reverential over the cement," and the rooms in which he couldn't sleep, "Sleep. But there is no sleep. A drunk is sobbing / In the hall. / Upstairs, an organ record / Of a Baptist hymn comes on. Past one o'clock."

In the early evening, after the galleries, I have my first chance. Hungry and wet, Beth, Elise, and I are in the mood for Indian food. We take the subway to Union Square and walk quickly to where Elise, with her outsized umbrella and beige thrift-store trenchcoat, has suggested we go: Curry Row. This whole visit, I have a folder of notes and maps in tow, keeping track of the Kees sites I need to see, and I realize we are about to walk by one now.

"Hey, Elise, hold up," I say as we're heading down a numbered avenue, about to cross East 10th Street. Beth and Elise agree to check it out with me; they know about the project. Elise thinks it's "neat," and Beth's offered to photograph all the buildings, and then there we are, Kees Site #1, not the first apartment he lived in in the city (actually, it's the fourth), but it's the first place I see: 129 East 10th Street on the block between Third and Second avenues, well in range of the bells of Saint Mark's, ringing as we approach.

Kees landed the place thanks to a connection through Ann, his wife, who was working for *Antiques* magazine. It was 1943 and one of the correspondents had to remain in the U.K. thanks to the war; an Atlantic crossing would have been too dangerous. The Keeses got to sublet her furnished apartment in a neighborhood their friend Janet Richards said had the aura of a "decayingly elegant cul de sac . . . with mossy homes from the Eighties." The windows were filigreed with vines and ferns and faced Saint Mark's. "There was an alcove," Richards said, "just big enough for a little Jacobean dining table. There was a kitchen that was only a short hallway between the alcove and the bathroom and . . . Ann washed the dishes in the bathroom sink. In the living room there were two single beds, covered with faded brocades, one against the wall, the other in the middle of the room, since there was no other place for it . . . and all of the furniture, the chairs, bookcases, little chests and tiny tables were relics of the eighteenth century, inconspicuously maintaining their unalterable perfection of design. On the floor was an ancient Oriental rug." The writer James Agee visited them there often, and they moved in just in time to impress Kees's parents when they came to town for an October visit.

Of course, I can't tell any of this from looking at the place, from the brick sidewalk on which I am standing outside the building's doorway. I jot in my notebook as Beth snaps away with her Nikon. Elise has wandered up the block to watch the tourists flock around Saint Mark's; it is a holiday weekend so there are a lot of them. Everything I know about this building and what may or may not have transpired in it I know from my research. From the outside, the building looks more or less like all the rest on the block, a gentrified residence in the East Village of the twenty-first century. It has six floors, iron lattices on the windows, and black iron balustrades. I don't even know what floor he lived on, and the odds are good I never will. I want it to be the third floor, though, because that is the one that is amber and lamp-lit with off-white curtains, curtains like the one Kees wrote that Ann made. A car with huge woofers drives by, playing slow bass, and an impatient guy honks for someone in the building next door.

"Are you done yet?" Beth asks, having waited patiently for fifteen minutes. "Let's go get some curry."

And I guess that I am done, for now, with this one. We walk on. This first stop wasn't a disappointment, but it wasn't totally satisfying. *But*, I tell myself as we walk down a narrow street lined with Indian restaurants whose owners stand in front wheedling for patrons, *I've only just begun.*

I've heard the voice of Weldon Kees, smooth and deep, on a recording he made of his original songs. I imagine him using it to recite: "This is the castle then, my dear, / With its justly famous view. / There are other historic sights in store— / Battlegrounds, parks we might explore, / The hundreds of monuments to war; / Now that you've seen the castle, my dear, / We'll see them before we're through."

That is what I intend to do: see his castles, see their views. I still think that if I map out his reckless trajectory, it might spell out some kind of message, like Nicholas Hawksmoor's churches in London or the Nazca Lines of Peru.

After our massive dinner—Beth haggled with the owner to throw in dessert with our vegetarian special, which already came with appetizers and a free bottle of wine—we strike off to a bar.

The rest of our visit will be the nonstop pastiche of subway rides, walks, drinks, restaurants, restrooms, museums, and friends we came here for, and will make me feel like a raw nerve in a wonderful way. But the major points of interest, the parts that will stand out the most, are the subsequent Kees sites. Weldon and Ann lived in the city from 1943 to 1950, but I will not visit the spots in chronological order; rather I will see them in the order I come upon them, hitting them when I go to visit living people and do living people things. But each site will fill me with a little thrill, like I'm collecting items for a scavenger hunt, like I'm catching ghosts out of the corners of my eyes.

Sunday is an idle Kees-spotting day; I see none of his rooms, rooms that he might call "dwarfed, immutable, and bare." But Monday morning, the chase is back on. The next point in the dartboard—Kees Site #2—is the Hotel Albert, a place where Kees didn't live, technically, but where he and Ann stayed when they came to visit with his Nebraskan parents in 1939 for the New York World's Fair. Kees chose the hotel—23 East 10th at the corner of University Place—for a reason that makes perfect sense to me: Hart Crane had a furnished room, from 1919 to 1920. The building—five sumptuous stories with bright green awnings—is not a hotel anymore. It contains luxury apartments and a Dean & DeLuca gourmet food store on the ground floor.

I'm not sure where to picture him here, among the old brick structures with molded windows and potted shrubs. I try to imagine whether the same smells, fetid and sour, would have been on the breeze, if that's what he was thinking when he wrote, "this rank wind / Blows through your rooms, untenanted." The trees stick up as spare as rakes—they have no leaves—and the side-walks are littered with orange peels and receipts. There is probably way more plastic on the ground now than when Kees was here with his parents. I know he loved being here from way out in the middle of nowhere, from Denver, where he was stuck in the Rockies, working in a library. Kees made it to New York for real before he turned thirty. I'm twenty-six. I resist the way this city acts as though if something doesn't happen here, then it doesn't happen, but I can't convince myself that Tacoma is really where I'm meant to be.

Kees's biographer, James Reidel, writes of how Kees could have taken, if he had wanted to, a professorial position at a university since his first book of poetry, *The Fall of the Magicians*, came out with a major press when he was just thirty-three. But Kees was determined to reject that career path; instead, he wrote in his satiric novel, *Fall Quarter*, of "the bad dream [he] imagined his life would be had he become a young college professor." To my dismay, it seems that I am living that dream, locked away in a back-biting backwater while the action happens elsewhere.

Beth snaps away with her Nikon.

I have no idea which way to look at Kees Site #3, lower Fifth Avenue and 10th Street. The directions are vague. "We have a remarkably cool apartment on lower Fifth Avenue and 10th Street"—a letter from Kees in July 1943—is all I have to go on. It's the same street, at any rate, that Emma Lazarus lived on, where she was a "Poet, Essayist, and Humanitarian" as the helpful blue plaque with white letters tells us. This is also the same street that Dawn Powell lived on, another literary Midwesterner come to the

big city, now all but forgotten. "The past goes down and disappears," Kees writes, "The present stumbles home to bed, / The
future stretches out in years / That no one knows, and you'll be
dead." You'll be dead, but someone you never knew might still
love you in spite—or because—of it.

It is Martin Luther King Jr. Day today. Tom was looking at a
book of photo essays about him this morning at the kitchen table,
and now a black man in a minivan with faux wood paneling is
listening to "I Have a Dream" turned up so high, you can hear it
through the closed windows.

Picture Kees here if you want, I tell myself. *He doesn't care.
Picture him anywhere in the city—he got around. Picture him, if
you want, in Mexico.*

Then off we go again to the sound of construction drills. I
wonder if the city sounded this way in his day too, if a city is
always in the process of becoming?

Kees Site #4 is much the same, the directions nebulous. "In
June, the Keeses moved back to East 10th Street, subletting from
Dwight and Nancy MacDonald, who were at the Cape for the
summer," says the Reidel biography. But this lack of specificity is
probably all right, because precision isn't exactly what's significant anyway. These buildings are in some ways like people, like
strangers; their interiorities are not available to me so I have to
use my eyes and my imagination, to size them up the way people
keep sizing up Beth and me, the women scanning: shoes, coat,
purse; the men scanning: legs, tits, face.

I know from letters Kees wrote about the place, whichever one it is, that it had "wonderful quiet," tropical fish, and

bookshelves "topheavy on Marxism," as well as a Steinway grand that he liked to play. I know I could, if I chose, infuse every window and doorway in my line of sight with meaning— maybe he touched that railing, sat on those stairs, or smoked on that fire escape. Because now that he must be dead, regardless of what happened to him that day in July of 1955, and because of the way he vanished, nothing in his life or work can ever be strictly as it seems. Everything becomes a symbol, a coded message. Donald Justice, an early Kees revivalist, himself now dead, writes in the introduction to *The Collected Poems*, "If the whole of poetry can be read as a denial of the values of the present civilization, as I believe it can, then the disappearance of Kees becomes as symbolic an act as Rimbaud's flight or Crane's suicide." Little facts and details become seemingly fraught, "These bilious things, fracturing / the night's surface, swerve / into graphs, hanging like crags in jagged lines: / —profound, perfect, and / not without meaning."

In spite of the rain and in spite of the stink, we are happy to be here, Beth and me, because the city is such an eyewash, such a visual change.

On our way to meet a friend for lunch at a Thai place, we come within striking distance of another Kees bonus site, not unlike the former Hotel Albert, although he and Ann visited this one while they were actually living here: Saint Vincent's Hospital at 144 West 12th Street, a part of the structure that became the Jacob L. Reiss Pavilion in 1955, the year Kees vanished, six floors high and with a delicate view of the ornate white building across the street.

I jot in my notebook and Beth snaps away with her Nikon. She has begun a series, abandoned Christmas trees, since everyone appears to be throwing theirs away this week, dry and brittle at the curbside next to the NY RECYCLES bins. Saint Vincent's is the site where, when he and Ann were returning from a 1947 trip to the Cape, their car, an ancient Plymouth they named Tiresias, caught fire. "You should have seen Weld's blistered thumb," wrote Ann. Dylan Thomas would die at Saint Vincent's in 1953.

We have time, before lunch, for one more stop, Kees Site #5: 152 South 7th Street, at the corner of Charles Street near Sheridan Square. Kees had been writing for *Time* magazine, but in September of 1943, he returned from a week's vacation to learn that he—and several other men who seemed on the brink of being drafted—had been "suddenly canned." A pacifist, skeptical of the use of war of any kind, Kees had long been wary of what he saw as a patriotism that was frequently blind and mindless. "The men who were haters of war are mounting the platforms," he writes in "June 1940." "An idiot wind is blowing and the conscience dies."

There are still UNITED WE STAND signs and American flags all over the city, more than five years after 9/11, and headlines call out from the newspaper bins about the deaths today—soldier and civilian—in Iraq and Afghanistan. Justice writes that Kees "is one of the bitterest poets in history," and that "the bitterness may be traced to a profound hatred for a botched civilization, Whitman's America come to a dead end on the shores of the Pacific."

Ann and Weldon lived on 7th for only a month before they found a more "'commodious and quieter' place that would not shock Weldon's parents when they arrived from Beatrice for a visit in early October." In the meantime, Kees was "lovingly placed in classification 4F" by the selective service office, perhaps for "defects above the neck" or perhaps just because he was "a man with a slight build who said he wrote poetry."

Something about this place looks especially sad, romantic, and dilapidated, even in a neighborhood that today seems upscale, even though there is a Sawa Sushi on the ground floor and a store called Khazam; and there are jingling dogtags on purebred dogs, mammoth Escalades, and streamlined strollers with lattes in the cup-holders pushed by skinny women clad all in black. There is a sex shop up the block called the Pleasure Chest. A bus pulls up and tourists, bundled up and doughy in their puffy jackets, throng at the entrance but hesitate to enter, as if they've never before seen this sort of emporium. Beth snaps away with her Nikon, taking pictures of them taking pictures of the sign above the door and the merchandise in the windows. "What the hell?" she says. "It's just a sex shop—it's not like there isn't a porn barn and a gentlemen's club by every truck stop in the United States."

I wonder about the grim and dingy interior of the apartment when Kees lived here: "This is your familiar room, / With your familiar odor lingering and real, / The known disturbance in the hall, / Worn rug, the broken chandelier, / The flowered paper peeling from the walls." I wonder what he smelled like. Soap? Cigarette smoke? Brillantine? Despair and hope and tailored fabrics? There is a Charles Food across the street. I know Kees liked to drink, but what did he eat?

After we eat, Beth and I (sort of) locate the last Kees site—#6—that we'll see today. We head to Union Square to hunt for the "flophouse" where he flopped after another move in 1948, a furnished room where he and Ann stayed until they could fix up another, more permanent place, an old factory that they and another couple would renovate and share.

I lack an exact address, but regardless, out of all the rest so far this area must look the most changed with its DSW, its Filene's, its Forever 21, and its Strawberry—with all its teeny-bopper clothing shops, shoe stores, and fast cafés. Beth doesn't know what building to photograph for me, so she stands in the center of the square at the base of a statue of a man on horseback and shoots 360 degrees, a circular panorama, just in case. There's nothing else to do but stop at a Starbucks to pee before we hop the subway to a dive bar in the Financial District to meet more old friends, some from the city, some in from Jersey.

I wonder if I would love him the same if he hadn't vanished. All I know about him now is all I will ever know. I haven't learned anything about him that can make me stop loving him, and I am never going to stop. He can do no wrong. He is perfect in my mind, frozen in time, "one of the last great romantics," his novelist friend, Anton Myrer described him. "He genuinely believed that sensibility and talent would receive due recognition with time."

The death of a poet—not just in a Lit Crit, death-of-the-author way, but literally, the fact of a poet's no longer being alive in the world—does not merely make that author's work *seem* better; rather it actually *makes* their work better. These details of the author's life and death are, like language itself, the material and the medium of which the work is comprised.

Well-respected dead poets, it seems, almost always enjoy a higher status than well-respected living ones. For instance, if you know that a particular poet is dead, you know too that he or she is probably not going to do something later that will embarrass you for liking them. Nor will he or she keep writing the same poem over and over so the impact is dulled. Nor will he or she produce work that is so obviously bad it causes you to question— and actually reduces—the value of earlier work.

By making all utterances more significant because of their finality, death—particularly death at one's own hand in the bloom of relative youth—gives poets the voice of authority, permitting them to say whatever they want. Ultimately, this power has to do with separateness, since separateness is part of the condition to which much of what we consider art aspires. If you as an artist intend to comment authoritatively on something—anything—you have the best chance of doing so from outside, free of all earthly entanglements. So you see, Weldon Kees is perfectly free, trapped though he often felt in what I know of his life.

The next two Kees sites, #7 and #8, I locate alone on Tuesday. Beth has her appointments with photo editors, so I take my own crappy digital camera with me. The rain has finally stopped and the weather's snapped cold, though it still doesn't feel quite cold enough. This is not the January Kees wrote of in a poem of that name, this is not a "Morning: blue, cold, and still" with "the wedge of light / At the end of the frozen room / Where snow on a windowsill, / Packed and cold as a life / Winters the sense of wrong / And emptiness and loss." Hesitant snow falls from the low gray sky, the flakes like mistakes not confidently made.

I take the subway to the seventh apartment, 227 East 25th Street, the place Ann and Weldon had to move to when the correspondent from *Antiques* made it back across the sea in November 1943. Howard Nemerov tipped them off to the place, as he was apartment hunting too with his new bride. Working class and noisy at the time Kees arrived, this place was nearby the Third Avenue El when it still existed. Kees called it a "noisebox" and said it "combined the poorer features of Grand Central Station, Ebbetts Field, Bellevue and the Chatauqua Bell Ringers."

Today, the apartment—five stories, cream-colored, with enormous fire escapes—seems bustling yet tucked away, next door to the Ninth Church of Christ, Scientist. Trucks go by, lumbering and encumbered, impatient cabs behind them. A tattered wreath with a red bow still hangs above the entryway. Depressions in the sidewalk, wet with yesterday's rain, have begun to freeze around the edges. I love Kees and I love his poems for their revelations and incisive satire, and for the precision of his imagery and for the turns of phrase that seem to me cold and sharp: "Like spines of air, frozen in an ice cube."

I stand across the street and watch people come and go. Even if I could get inside, I still wouldn't know which apartment to look in. And I know that even if I did, I'd be as likely to see Kees as I would his character Robinson, his poetic alter ego. A dead man is just as absent—just as invented—as the man who never existed in the first place. "The mirror from Mexico, stuck to the wall, / Reflects nothing at all," writes Kees in "Robinson." "The glass is black. / Robinson alone provides the image Robinsonian. // Which is all of the room—walls, curtains, / Shelves, bed, the tinted photograph of Robinson's first wife, / Rugs, vases, panatelas in a humidor. / They would fill the room if Robinson came in. // The pages in the books are blank, / The books that Robinson has read. That is his favorite chair, / Or where the chair would be if Robinson were here."

I walk down the street, past the American Academy of Pet Grooming, a psychic's, and a clutch of low colorful buildings with laundry hanging out the windows—red, blue, yellow. I meet a friend for lunch in Koreatown, then head to Kees Site #8, 31 East 30th Street, where he first lived, alone, in 1943, moving in from a room at the Chelsea Hotel. Separated from Ann at the time, he chose the spot because it was furnished, convenient, close to the Fifth Avenue offices of Russell & Volkening, his literary agency, where they let him use a typewriter. Now that I've seen this place, another short-ish brick building, much like the others, there will be only two more spots left to locate.

Ultimately, my haphazard yearning to be where Kees used to be, to see what he saw, is unappeasable. None of these spots are the same as they were, or maybe they simultaneously are even as they are not. It's like that philosophical paradox, the Ship of Theseus: when Theseus returned to Athens having saved the Athenian youth and slain the Minotaur, the Athenians were so grateful, they kept his ship as a monument in the harbor. As the ship decayed, they replaced its planks, until none of the original timber remained. Was it still the Ship of Theseus? The whole city is this way. It *is* New York and yet it's *not*. "The ruined structures cluttering the past, / a little at a time and slow is best . . ."

Snowflakes fall like ash from a cigarette. I am blocking the sidewalk. I am in the way. I miss Beth and I want to tell somebody about what I've just thought, but none of these pedestrians gives a fuck about Theseus or Kees. Why should they? I take the subway uptown. I go to the Frick.

While I am there, looking at art, alone, listening to the commentary on my audio-guide, I notice: one of the guards looks like Weldon Kees. Thin, slight, not much taller than me, his dark hair swept back, he wears tailored slacks and a uniform jacket. I keep looking at him in a way I think is discreet, but evidently isn't. He catches me staring so often, he comes over and asks if I need anything. I smile and say no, then he smiles back and asks if I have plans that evening because he gets off at five, and I say thanks, but no and extricate myself politely.

The next morning, Wednesday, we wake up early, the same time as Elise who has to be at work in the shipping department at Christie's by nine. When I peek out the curtain on the way to the shower, the sky is as clear and blue as a very blue sky. It is cold again, and finally feels like January. Beth and I have been and gone and done and seen until all that's left of our visit are two packed suitcases and one unmade bed, and a little trail of Kees site pushpins in my mental map of the city. There are only two left to stick in: one in Brooklyn and one kind of near Chinatown, which is where we are and where we're headed anyway, to catch the Fung Wah Bus from lower Manhattan to Boston.

These last two stops will turn out to be the most arduous. We hug Tom and Elise good-bye, luggage in tow, as they lock the door behind us. According to my research, the apartment in Brooklyn was the place Kees moved to after the East 10th Street sublet from the MacDonalds ran out. "This time they looked in

Brooklyn Heights, since they had heard that the neighborhood, with its handsome brownstones, was quiet and affordable." Hart Crane had lived in the area "with a rooftop view of the span that inspired his long poem 'The Bridge,'" a piece of Brooklyn trivia which Kees had liked.

Brooklyn Heights, we discover, is not especially easy to get to from Greenpoint. We take three trains, hike up and down a ridiculous number of stairs, go against the flow in the middle of rush hour, and have to ask a sweet old lady for directions, but eventually we get there. The neighborhood *is* handsome, full of brownstones and quiet, though as for affordable, we guess not anymore. Elise told us they used to film *The Cosby Show* here, and that looks about right: homey houses with prominent stoops. She said that movies were shot here too, that you'd walk by in the summer and see signs with various film companies' names and the message "Rain Machines Operating from ___ to ___" containing the dates.

Kees Site #9—144 Willow Street, a beautiful structure on a street lined with Federal-style buildings—is now a residence hall for students of the Brooklyn Law School. Whichever apartment was his, I know it "was on a floor high enough for them to have a view of the harbor if they went out on the balcony," and that it had a living room big enough for the Knoll furniture they took out of storage, as well as for Kees's paintings and a small art studio.

It is so bright and so cold and so clear today that it is hard for me to believe that they—Weldon and Ann, and even Hart Crane—were sad all the time. *Because they were not*, I remind myself. *Sometimes, they were happy*. Looking at this place makes me happy too, and I wonder if these were the rooms about which he wrote "Late Evening Song": "For a while / Let it be enough: / The responsive smile, / Though effort goes into it. // Across the warm room / Shared in candlelight, / This look beyond shame, / Possible now, at night // Goes out to yours."

"Can we go yet?" says Beth, Nikon around her neck, rubbing her fingers in her fingerless gloves. "It's freezing out here."

We emerge one last time from the subway into the light of Canal Street in Chinatown, as close as we'll get to the one Kees site I wasn't able to find, the converted factory at 179 Stanton Street. Kees Site #10—the last place on my list and, fittingly, the last place in the city he and Ann lived before leaving in 1950—was, according to the biography, "in the 'lox and bagel section' of the Lower East Side, running just north of and parallel to Canal Street." But based on MapQuest and GoogleMaps, I couldn't figure out how to get to the street easily that day—it was not parallel to Canal at all, it turns out, but farther north and east, parallel to Delancey.

If the place were still standing, which I have reason to doubt, I might have seen that it was fifty feet long, with thirteen windows. The tenant prior to the Keeses and their friends the Myrers had been a designer who left nasty adhesives and modeling clay behind her. It took the two couples forever to get her junk down four flights of steep stairs. Even post-restoration, Ann called it "a barn" with "practically none of the comforts of home except hot water and a toilet, but lots of windows which I count whenever I'm feeling depressed about the gallons of paint we slapped on this place." There was no phone, so Kees got his messages at the

Peridot, his art gallery. That winter, from 1949 to 1950, seemed to both of them the worst of their lives.

As we walk along Canal, I picture the old factory as a place where Kees felt "Nailed up in a box, / Nailed up in a pen, nailed up in a room / That once enclosed you amiably, you write, 'Finished. No more. The end,' signing your name. / Frantic, but proud of penmanship"; where he felt "These rooms of ours are those that rock the worst. / Cold in the heart and colder in the brain, / We blink in darkened rooms toward exits that are gone."

Weldon and Ann made their exit from the city in such a hurry that when Ann remembered she'd left cookbooks in the kitchen of a friend, Weldon refused to turn back.

Walking up Canal Street, wheeling my luggage behind me, I am not in a hurry, though I am excited about Boston. I am sorry to be leaving New York already, sorry too that this means I'm that much closer to having to go back to Tacoma. Beth and I stop at a crosswalk. There are two man-sized footprints, full of ice, in the cement at my feet: shoes, not boots, stylish and belonging to a smallish man. They cannot have been made by Kees, but I wish they could have, and I wonder if he ever stood here. I have found some things, but none of them holdable; "I have come back / As empty-handed as I went."

DID YOU ASK
FOR THE
HAPPY ENDING?

*T*HE OLYMPIC GAME Farm is where retired Disney animal actors go to die. Or, if you prefer, to live out their days.

Kathleen's husband, a novelist, says if you write something in the third person, then it is automatically fiction. She would prefer that the following experience not really have happened, so she thinks of it this way. She imagines herself being narrated as if on film.

Located at the remote end of what used to be a remote village at the base of the Olympic Mountains on Washington state's westernmost peninsula, the Olympic Game Farm used to be a private filming and training facility for four-legged stars of both the small and silver screens. Kathleen imagines how various scenes from her visit there might play with test audiences and tries to come up with alternatives and options.

ESSAY INTRODUCTION A:

The Olympic Game Farm in Sequim, Washington, is not so much a petting zoo as it is a breading zoo.

The girl at the gate emerges from the dilapidated ranger hut and sells them a stale loaf of Western Farms Wheat Bread for a flat two dollars. Before she does, though, she hands Kathleen the map of the driving tour and tells them the rules. This is a family-run operation, the map explains with pride, and Kathleen wonders if maybe she's the owner's granddaughter.

"You must stay completely inside your automobile at all times. If you come out of your vehicle, you will be kicked from the farm.

"You must keep your doors, large windows, and sunroofs closed. If you open any of those, you will be kicked from the farm.

"When you drive through the exhibit containing the buffalos, you must keep your vehicle moving or else the animals will come up, surround you, and box you in. They may damage your vehicle, and we will have to come save you, and you will be kicked from the farm.

"Watch your fingers."

Kathleen eyes up the admission rates as they drive by the peeling kiosk.

ESSAY INTRODUCTION B:

Kathleen's mother has a tendency to read roadside signs aloud. "SEQUIM VIEW CEMETERY," she dictates, and "JUBILEE FARMS," "THE DUNGENESS RIVER," "FIRST BAPTIST CHURCH OF SEQUIM," and "SEVENTH DAY ADVENTISTS," and so on and on the whole ride down to the Olympic Game Farm from what used to be the center of a very small town. "PURPLE HAZE LAVENDER FARM" and "WEANER PIGS" and "HORSES TO RENT," she reads as they roll along.

Powerlines sag in front of farmland being sold for conversion to crowded lots that will eventually contain single-family homes. Small blackbirds line these lines, looking like notes on a musical staff. If you played them, Kathleen imagines, they would chirp,

"Little boxes on the hillside, / Little boxes made of ticky-tacky, / Little boxes, little boxes, / Little boxes, all the same."

This is the farthest west Kathleen has ever been and she is finding this portion of it disappointingly unwild. Kathleen is a professor at a small religious university farther down the more populous end of Puget Sound and she is on spring break. Her Midwestern parents had never seen the Pacific Northwest, so they have come to visit her. They've all taken a road trip out to the peninsula.

Kathleen gets depressed by zoos, is depressed by Sequim with its property-rights fanatics and its colossally irresponsible lack of zoning. She is trying hard not to have a bitchy, thirteen-year-old adolescent mindset, full of resentment and deadly boredom.

She slouches in the front seat, next to her husband Martin, who is driving. Her mother and father, dressed in light, mail-order raincoats fresh from L.L.Bean and Cabela's, sit upright in the back. Kathleen and Martin's outerwear and hiking boots are several years old owing to their tendency to need to spend their money on things like rent, food, and staggering student loans. Martin rolls down the driver's-side window to listen to the pale girl with the strange eyebrows and the nose ring tell them the official rules of the park.

Kathleen eyes the rates as they drive by the peeling kiosk:

WINTER ADMISSION RATES:

ADULTS 13 & OVER: $9.00
YOUTH: 6 THRU 12: $8.00
SENIORS OVER 60: $9.00
AGES 4 & 5: $1.00
3 YEARS AND UNDER: FREE

How is thirteen adult? And how am I one? I am twice that age and I still do not feel like someone old enough to shell out nine bucks to get in here.

If they were alone, Kathleen would say this aloud to Martin, but she does not want to be an ingrate to her parents. Then again, if they were alone, Kathleen and Martin would not be here among the B-movie animal actors in the first place. Nor, she thinks, trying to accentuate the positive, would they be able to afford vacationing on the beautiful Olympic Peninsula at all.

"I'm so glad we found the time to stop by here before you guys had to head back home," Kathleen says, smiling at her parents via the small, square mirror set into the sun visor.

NECESSARY EXPOSITIONAL DIALOGUE ABOUT SETTING A:

It is late March, still the rainy season farther down the Puget Sound in Seattle, in Tacoma, but here the sun had shone without fail for the past three days.

"As much as I hate to see it," Kathleen's mother opines from the backseat, "you can really understand why so many people would want to move up here."

Sequim bills itself rightly as a geographic wonder, situated fortuitously in the heart of the Dungeness Valley beneath what was known in meteorology as a Blue Hole. Though clouds bank high on both sides of the deep, green bowl, the skies over Sequim remain, for the most part, preternaturally blue.

"Yeah," says Kathleen. "Who doesn't like the sunshine?"

EXPOSITIONAL DIALOGUE ABOUT SETTING B:

FOR SALE signs feature on fence after fence, often listing explicitly the cost of the house or the piece of property.

"It's a good thing you and Martin are trying to save money," her dad opines. "It's too bad a person can't get out and travel as much as they'd like when they're young, but I guess that's just the way it is. You pay your dues."

"Mmm-hmm," Kathleen murmurs, reading silently in the guidebook. Because Sequim is located downwind of the mountains, it exists in a rain shadow. The precipitation in the valley amounts to just fifteen inches per year compared to, for example, more than one hundred and fifty in the Hoh Rainforest on the other side of the Olympics. This is why so many people want to live in Sequim, to build their second homes there if they are middle-aged or to retire and die there if they are wealthy retirees.

Kathleen hates this attitude and hates these inhabitants, erecting their McMansions, their WalMarts, their Home Depots, and their Applebee's; driving their SUVs in the woods, ATVs on the beaches, private planes in the skies, and jetskis in the sea; eating all the salmon and the Dungeness crab, drinking all the water, and cutting down the trees.

ACT 1, VERSION A:

"AQUARIUM—CLOSED," reads Kathleen's mother from the backseat as they drive through the entrance, past the collapsing circular shack stenciled with trout, perch, and bass.

The car bounces down a dirt and gravel path that looks exactly as it must have when the park opened to the public in 1972.

According to the upbeat promotional guide magazine provided by the bureau of tourism, founder Lloyd Beebe was a logger whose family moved to Sequim during the Great Depression. Beebe worked long and perilous hours as a logger before achieving the American dream of owning his own place in 1942. The farm started out dairy, but quickly turned game once Beebe, an amateur photographer and filmmaker, was able to interest one Walt Disney in his footage.

"The peacocks sound like they're meowing," says Kathleen's father, and he is right.

Far away at first, then nearby, peahens squawk out begging cries. Kathleen opens the transparent orange cellophane surrounding the bread, and hands around the spongy slices.

"Look at that one, Kath," her father taps her on the shoulder with his digital camera. "He's a big guy—get a picture."

She obliges. The bird is so close, the resulting image has an eerie fish-eye effect. Her father, a hunter, as avid about getting shots of some animals as he is about shooting others, is pleased. Kathleen smiles to see him so happy. He is almost old enough to merit the senior winter rate.

Past the peacocks near the pond just beyond the gate lies a fork in the road.

ACT 1, VERSION B:

Steel cages and cropped dry grass. Huge fences to keep animals in and people out. Kathleen would rather not see this—all these washed-up animals, too tame for the wild, too special for the zoo, and the spread itself, once a sign of the fruits of big-time ambition, now the site of a dream that has ceased coming true. She takes a chipped compact from her purse. Her bright red lipstick has faded, eaten mostly away with breakfast earlier that morning at the B and B.

Passing the derelict aquarium, she sees a few other guests. Maybe it's the setting, but they look to her like people from the '70s, Californians from the old Drivers' Ed filmstrips she learned to steer to in high school back in Illinois. They look like people who may, to this day, in the privacy of their own homes, watch *The Life and Times of Grizzly Adams*, both the movie and the TV series, as well as other films that were either shot on the grounds or whose stars reside here now, arthritic at their joints, grizzled at their muzzles. People who might be genuinely entertained by such works as 1973's *Seems There Was This Moose*, 1971's *Lefty the Ding-A-Ling Lynx*, *Charlie the Lonesome Cougar* from 1967, or *The Outlaw Cats of Colossal Cave* from 1975. If Kathleen can be said to enjoy these films, it is only the result of her reliance on hefty amounts of irony.

Beebe's break of a lifetime, the one that made all that now spreads before Kathleen possible, came in 1949 with the short film *The Little Archer*, starring his telegenic and cooperative five-year-old son Melvin.

Kathleen reads the plot summary aloud to her family:

"The little boy, quite skilled with his bow and arrows, sets out on a hunting trip after kissing his mother good-bye. He hadn't gone too far when he encountered a fawn. Now, that's too pretty an animal to shoot, so he continues on his way. Before too long, little Melvin sees a bear cub sitting on a stump. He takes deadly aim with his bow and arrow, then has second thoughts as the cub gets off the stump and ambles over to him.

"Since the bear is a friendly sort, the little boy and the bear sit down and eat the lunch Melvin's mother has packed for him.

Lunch finished, Melvin continues his journey. Before too long, he spies a cougar cub, who joins in the fun of this parade of youngsters, all of who [sic] return home with the archer to continue their play in the yard at the house. At this point, our intrepid hunter puts on a demonstration of his shooting prowess for the benefit of all who will watch."

"Wow," says Martin.

"What a sweet story," says her mother.

"How much did the old guy sell it for?" asks her dad.

"*The Little Archer* sold to Warner Brothers for $2,000," Kathleen reads. "This in turn opened the door for a working relationship with Disney."

"That was a lot of money back in the forties," her dad nods approvingly.

When the peacocks approach their vehicle, the animals look grainy and televised, a story you'd see on the kind of TV with a dot glowing in the center long after you've turned it off.

Kathleen wads the first slice, the heel of the loaf, into tiny round pellets, the better to hurl them directly into the beaks of the waiting peacocks, blue and bold; the better to avoid the swarming seagulls, looking to freeload.

They come to a fork in the trail, one high and one low.

Buses, Kathleen sees on the double-sided page of rules, must take the lower road; cars can take whichever one they please. "I don't think it matters," she says, adding *they both go nowhere* in her mind before suggesting brightly, "Let's take the high one. It has prairie dogs and llamas."

Up they go.

MONTAGE FOR EFFICIENCY'S SAKE A:

This sequence should be set to music, something upbeat and zany; wacky in a Benny Hill "Yakety Sax" kind of vein to convey that Kathleen is being won over in spite of herself.

Prairie dogs—fat, pear-shaped, and slow—peep out of the holes in their dusty "town."

The llamas are fearless, peering into the vehicle with large limpid eyes and much curiosity.

"Careful you don't get spit on," Kathleen's mother laughs from the backseat as Martin hands the bravest llama a whole slice of whole wheat.

"Roll up your window!" Kathleen squeals as the llama tries to stick his entire upper body into the driver's side. The beast begins to gallop alongside the vehicle, slobbering, almost smiling as the passengers inside scream with delight.

Next up: the white rhino—ghostly, mythic.

Then: Roosevelt's Elk. "They're special," her dad admires. "They're smaller than normal elk. Cute little guys."

The arctic foxes prance fluffily, the Bengal tigers seem to dance, and the wolves howl at the cloudless sky. The cougars roar and the buffalos drool and stink.

Kathleen's heart melts, you can see it in her face—she is beginning to have a good time. She thinks fondly of childhood family vacations to other let's-interact-and-make-learning-fun locations, including but not limited to the Wisconsin Dells and the Ozark Village in Branson, Missouri.

She can't help but think of the majesty and promise of America, her country, as they pull up to the bear exhibit.

MONTAGE FOR EFFICIENCY'S SAKE B:

This sequence should be silent, documentary-style.

Even when he follows Kathleen's advice to throw the bread chunks into their burrows, Martin can't help the waddling prairie dogs compete with the interloping gulls. Even the filthy, gray, mottled, one-legged seabirds outpace the pudgy mammals.

Kathleen is not having the best of times. The white rhino looks bored. The King David's deer are also mysterious and white. The big mystery, though, is: Why are they here? And how long will they be? What do they feel and what do they—can they?—think? Do they hate their pens? Does their own stink bother them?

"See how the metal pipes, those grates between pens, keep the animals from walking from one section to another? They don't like to walk on that metal with their hooves," her dad explains, pointing.

Kathleen reads silently, "The driving tour leaves our visitors with vivid memories of these amazing creatures. Experiences which at first are hard to imagine become pleasantly surprising . . ."

Looking up, Kathleen realizes they have already arrived at the bear exhibit.

Kathleen has heard of but never seen the film or the series *The Life and Times of Grizzly Adams*, but this is the show on which this game farm hangs its reputation. Ben the Bear is their bread and butter. Yet looking out over the grimy sea of grizzlies, it is impossible to tell which one he is.

CLIMACTIC BEAR-FEEDING SCENE A:

Here, Kathleen and her companions go through half a loaf of bread with great rapidity. Many of the grizzlies are too lazy to bother getting up to chase the torn chunks, but the ones who do, more than make up for their sleepy pen-mates.

"Look at those claws, those teeth!" her mother cries.

"Boy, the seagulls sure steer clear of these guys, don't they?" her father smiles.

Which grizzly is famous, wonders Kathleen. *And does he know it himself?* One of the bears, especially big and especially old-looking, seems to smile, to pose for the camera: purple tongue, yellow grin. She has read that grizzlies typically live fifteen to twenty-five years in the wild, but that in captivity, they can survive for well over thirty.

Is this one Ben? Kathleen doesn't care; she's just happy to be here.

CLIMACTIC BEAR-FEEDING SCENE B:

As the bread leaves her fingers, Kathleen tries to ensure that it flies directly into the waiting maw of the bear. She has noticed that he is too lackadaisical to pick up most of the earlier bits that landed in the slight ditch in front of him. Or perhaps his reluctance is not so much to do with ursine sluggishness, but rather with the fact that the morsels have landed a bit too close to the electric fence for comfort.

Kathleen has read that in the wild, grizzlies are naturally omnivorous, and that they will feed on moose, caribou, deer, and sheep—even other bears, black ones usually. Grizzlies also prey on fish such as salmon, trout, and bass. They will scavenge as well, but either way, they prefer a diet which consists predominantly of protein.

Why is Kathleen throwing the bread? How has she come to love these spectacles untutored, rude? When she was a kid, sure, okay, but what is she doing here now, now that she is a vegetarian in favor of animal rights, well-aware that this bread-tossing is unhealthy and dietarily imbalanced, not to mention sort of tasteless and déclassé?

REFLECTIVE SCENE BEFORE THE CONCLUSION A:

Before they leave the farm, they pass the peacock pond one final time, so they can unload the rest of their loaf. One particularly precocious seagull plants himself on the hood, dead center of the windshield, and refuses to move, even when the bread is gone and Martin throws the vehicle into reverse.

Kathleen imagines they are in a time machine with a seagull hood ornament, journeying back to an era when this kind of display counted as good family fun; an era when she didn't know any better, when the Olympic Game Farm could seem entertaining for everyone: man and beast.

REFLECTIVE SCENE BEFORE THE CONCLUSION B:

Kathleen does her best to overcome her queasiness as she helps get rid of the rest of the bread. She sort of hates herself for throwing the bread, even as she loves the animals eating it.

If the animals could conceive of a point of view, would they think of themselves in first person or third? First person plural, Kathleen guesses: we we we. Not: I I I, me me me, like humans. Where will the animals go when Sequim creeps out? When the owners die?

Kathleen never saw the Beebes, but feels she can relate to them. They never had huge success, the kind of which they clearly dreamed. Most people have never heard of them. Nature specials the likes of which Disney put together in the '50s and '60s have seen their heyday and are watched rarely at best. Kathleen fears this kind of low-grade success for herself in the future. It makes her want to choke herself to death on cheap whole wheat. Kathleen just turned twenty-seven, which is pretty close to thirty. She'd probably be dead by now if she were a grizzly.

If she were alone with Martin, she'd say this aloud and they'd laugh. Her parents would fail to see the humor, though, and more than that, she wants them to be able to believe that she, Kathleen, is still a contender; that she still believes she can be anything she wants to be.

ESSAY CONCLUSION A:

Kathleen had been bummed out and depressed at the prospect of going into the Olympic Game Farm, but was touched by the unselfconscious simplicity of the animals there. Their youthful openness and easy candor rendered her more youthful and candid in her outlook until she was almost childlike and decidedly light-hearted going out.

While they wait for her parents to return from the restrooms at the front of the farm, Kathleen brushes breadcrumbs from the gray seat of their Ford Taurus, warmed already by these memories she'll keep for a lifetime.

As they loop back and head south, down to Tacoma, she feels blessed, blissed out, and back on track to her current home and pursuits.

ESSAY CONCLUSION B:

Kathleen had been bummed out and depressed at the prospect of going into the Olympic Game Farm, and she is even more bummed and depressed going out. She is touched by the animals, but deeply saddened by their trappedness.

Had they ever been free? Perhaps once, they had been hopeful, waiting for their big break, to break free of the cages and through to their potential, but all these gatekeepers, these jailers, these curtailers and crushers of their wildest dreams, keep them here. Perhaps they, like her, feel they are ready to burst at their seams, even as they know in their animal souls that they'll always stay stuck within their skins.

While they wait for her parents to return from the restrooms at the front of the farm, Kathleen brushes breadcrumbs from the gray seat of their used Ford Taurus, which they'd unexpectedly had to buy last Thanksgiving, when the ancient Hyundai they'd purchased off craigslist had broken down for the final time.

A bread tag mosaic, courtesy of littering tourists, lies—inadvertently pretty—along the path to the bathrooms. Two bantam chickens, a rooster and a hen, sit nestled near the corner of the white brick structure. The colorful birds are clearly getting nowhere fast, laying eggs that nobody has asked for or wants. It could be said there is no point to their product. But, Kathleen sees, they lay them anyway.

The rooster crows—earsplitting, loud—and the small hen clucks with what sounds like pride, as the family piles back into the car and drives away.

ALL
TOMORROW'S
PARTIES

"With great power comes great responsibility."

$\mathcal{S}$TEVIE HAD TURNED in her final portfolio for the Personal
Essay in a Spiderman folder with that quotation on the inside front pocket.

Kathy, her professor, thought of that advice as she sat on
the midnight blue couch between her student Charlie on her left
and her husband Martin on her right, in her student Audrey's
apartment.

Charlie was brash, a self-styled lady's man, full of bravado
and goofy panache. He was working class, but with academic
aspirations, from the city of Puyallup. He loved beer, women,
cars, and guitars, and would share that list with anyone who'd
listen. He drove a red Mustang convertible he'd fixed up himself, adored Stevie Ray Vaughan and deplored Jimmy Page. He'd
held a succession of crappy low-wage jobs in the automotive

departments of Sears and Sam's Club. He was bluff and swaggering, but the surface was thin, and his heart was good; anyone could see. All the girls in class were crazy for Charlie, but Kathy had suspected and recently had confirmed that Charlie was crazy only for Kathy.

The couch was velour. Audrey was the hostess. The couch was foldout. Audrey was throwing the cookout. The couch was big enough for exactly three people to sit comfortably without touching. Audrey was forcing everyone in attendance to eat Boca burgers because she and her roommate were both committed vegetarians, and could not abide the lingering stink of flesh in their house.

Last night, during their final class together, a debate had ensued: which superhero was cooler, Bat- or Spider-man?

"Bruce Wayne gets hotter women," Charlie pointed out.

"But Peter Parker gets MJ," Stevie shot back.

"Yeah," said Charlie, "but she wants a committed, emotionally involved relationship."

"What's wrong with that?" Stevie asked, her gangly hand landing with a slap on the white conference table.

Class was about to start. Kathy wanted to stay on track.

"Strictly speaking," she chimed in, "Batman was probably cooler, for whatever that's worth—the car, the gadgets, the toys, the money. But Spidey might ultimately be the better man. He was the underdog, the poor smart guy forced to make good—not a Dark Knight but a confused kid with the potential for greatness. Now who wants to go first in workshop tonight?"

After class that evening, Kathy had sat on the bed of the third-floor walk-up she shared with Martin, grading portfolios.

She had assigned final revisions instead of an exam, and had them write in-class self-evaluation letters assessing their progress. They were to discuss the top lessons they had learned about reading, writing, and revising. All the letters were honest and thoughtful, reflecting on their strengths, as well as their struggles. Most of them took up at least a full, crammed, handwritten page.

Charlie's portfolio was in a translucent green plastic folder. He labeled it boldly, with a Sharpie, in faux calligraphy "A Collection of Essays from a Sexy Man Beast." His letter, black ink on jagged loose-leaf, concluded with a second page, on which was written, super neatly: "Well, I was kind of debating on this, but since you're leaving, what the hell? You are a total babe as well, I mean, really hot."

Kathy's heart beat faster and she laughed out loud. She showed Martin.

"You *are* a total babe," he said and kissed her.

She decided not to let on at Audrey's party that she'd already read, and been flattered by, the letter.

Kathy liked Spiderman because he was vulnerable and because he took chances. He was the first adolescent superhero at a time when most teenage characters were cast as sidekicks. She'd read somewhere that Spidey's self-conscious obsessions with rejection, inadequacy, and loneliness made him less invincible and more relatable to younger readers, readers not unlike her twenty- and twenty-one- and twenty-two-year-old students. Readers not unlike her twenty-seven-year-old self.

Audrey's living room was ringed with extra chairs, and in the chairs sat the majority of students from that class. They sipped Blue Moon from the bottle as the sun beat in through the western-facing window. It lit Charlie from the side, set his profile on fire, and made his carefully disheveled hair shine bright as a halo. The light made Kathy squint when she turned that direction.

They were so far out west, all the way west, that the sun stayed up forever, it seemed. It didn't get dark until nine o'clock at least, now that it was May and the long gray rainy season was finally over.

"What was it like growing up here?" Kathy was asking her soon-to-be-former students. "When I was little, I never wanted to go to bed before it got dark out, but here you'd just about have to. You'd be doomed to it."

"It sucked growing up here. It still sucks now," said Charlie.

It was all set up to be an excellent party. A fridge full of beer; table full of food. Audrey had even put together a party mix to blare from the stereo. These soon-to-be-former students of Kathy's were all so happy to have her there. And she was happy too—happier, probably, than any of them knew—to be there.

Audrey's apartment was in Parkland, Washington. "The ghetto," her students called it. Normally, when she'd taught in Boston especially, Kathy corrected her students' use of this term.

When collegiate young people referred to something as "ghetto" it usually (a) was not, and (b) struck her as akin to calling something "gay" or "retarded."

Parkland was, though, ghetto: the fights, the shootings, the high concentration of an underprivileged class of people. So when her students here called Parkland "ghetto," Kathy would try to go for the teachable moment. Why, she would ask, was Parkland ghetto, and how did their small religious university manage to exist as a safe and sheltered bubble in the midst of so much need? The billboards in Parkland for a famous fast-food restaurant's one-dollar hamburgers, for example, read "Way Tastier than a Lotto Ticket," which she pointed out to her students as offensive. Why, she would ask, do some people in Parkland pay $23,000 a year to attend a small religious university, while others have to decide on a daily basis whether to eat or to gamble because their economic position is so desperately hopeless?

But the students from this class, the Personal Essay, never upset her by calling anything ghetto. And at this party, they were revealing even more about themselves and their lives than they had in their essays. A visiting assistant professor, Kathy was leaving the small religious university forever in a little over two weeks; her students had been candid in their writing before, but there was no need to hide anything now.

"I have a confession to make," Charlie said, turning to her. "I came to your class drunk one time. Or maybe twice."

"It happens," she said. "At least you came."

"Have you ever showed up drunk to teach?"

"Yes and no," she replied. "I taught an 8:00 A.M. last semester and once I showed up hungover, a little drunk from the night before."

This had been in the late fall, a long, dark period, which when she looked back on it, seemed in her mind to have been lit by candles or a flashlight: a dim, gloomy, and wet expanse of time punctuated by disappointment.

"That's not so bad," Charlie said and brought his bottle to his lips. "So like, the weirdest thing happened to me recently."

The party had broken down into smaller groups; Martin was chatting with Tabitha, comparing and contrasting anecdotes from their Texas upbringings.

"I slept with my girlfriend's—well, my ex, but she's not ex because of this—I slept with my ex-girlfriend's mom," Charlie said.

It was hard for Kathy to believe that Charlie had ended up at this small religious university at all, let alone in two of her classes, once in the fall and once in the spring. That he attended a university where other students said they would pray for her if they heard she had the sniffles. The same university where she would receive emails from students that said, "Hey Professor! Just working on my essay . . . is it okay to say 'doesn't do one darn of a good' and 'underoos' (instead of underwear)?" and then again, after that one, sent at 8:41 P.M., another at 8:42 which read in its entirety, "And what about 'give a toot'?"

"Really?" said Kathy, cocking her head. "And what did you think?"

"I thought it was great," said Charlie, eyes blurry, widening behind his black-framed glasses. "Crazy thing was, she was better than my girlfriend. And she was forty-six."

"Older women," smiled Kathy. "All that experience."

"I mean, I didn't want to hurt anybody. My girlfriend was kind of a bitch—stuck-up. I was going to dump her anyway." Sheepish, Charlie shrugged his plaid-clad shoulders up toward his ears, tousled brown hair curling around them, brown eyes staring into Kathy's without blinking.

"Anybody need a drink? Everybody doing okay?" Audrey emerged from the kitchen wielding a greasy spatula and wearing an apron.

"I meant to mention it before, but that box on the table is our vice box," she explained. "Me and Kirsten think it's funny to keep things in there that young ladies weren't supposed to do in college back in the day. There's cards and cigarettes. We were going to put condoms too, but we decided some people might find that gross. Also, it's not convenient. Help yourselves."

Stevie sprang from her chair to the wooden crate. Charlie and Kathy leaned forward in unison.

"Oooh! A clove?" squealed Stevie, pulling the battered black cigarette from the box and holding it aloft. "Audrey, can we have it?"

"Knock yourselves out."

The three of them filed through the screen door onto Audrey's balcony, Stevie in the lead, the gold band of the clove flashing in the sunlight.

"I haven't smoked one of these since I was probably nineteen," said Kathy.

"I know," said Stevie. "I haven't had one since boarding school in New York."

"I'll smoke anything," said Charlie, taking the first drag and passing it to Kathy, brushing her hand slightly. His fingertips were callused. Kathy took her puff and handed it to Stevie, who sucked theatrically, narrow cheeks collapsing, high cheekbones protruding.

"Now you've both made out with me by proxy," Charlie said and grinned, his straight strong teeth improbably white.

Martin came to the door and looked out. "And what are we doing here?" he asked Kathy disapprovingly. She had not smoked since January, at a party in Seattle, the thirtieth birthday of a blonde, outdoorsy friend, with chili peppers galore on RateMyProfessors.com. Since Kathy had quit smoking entirely, even socially, Martin was supposed to give her a hard time on the rare occasions she relapsed.

"We are doing what it looks like," Kathy said. "We are smoking. I'm sorry. I'm just having fun."

"All right, your choice," said Martin, and returned to his conversation.

Kathy used to reprimand the smokers in her Personal Essay class for taking too long to return from the break she gave at the midpoint of the evening: "Smoke 'em if you got 'em, but everybody be back in five, okay?"

On her way to the bathroom or to the water fountain, Kathy would look down to the quad from the huge windows on the second-floor balcony of the humanities building and see them: Brian in his leather jacket, Charlie in his color-change glasses that became shades in the sunlight, both in their tough guy postures, their youth elapsing even as they were in it. Even as they savored it, they hastened its end.

"I've wanted to ask you all semester, Kathy," Stevie was saying. "Why is it you don't drive?"

"Yeah," said Charlie, passing her the cigarette. "Driving's the best thing ever."

Kathy licked the gritty sweetness of the clove from her lower lip, and thought about her answer. "I've just never liked it. From day one of Drivers' Ed on, cars have seemed like death-traps to me. Like those movies they'd show you in health class about all the hideous ways you could get killed through reckless driving? Most people will tell you they're excellent drivers, but that can't be true. Not everyone can be exceptional. Me on the other hand, I'm an average driver. I'm fidgety—I like to look at maps and play with the radio. Also, because I hate driving so much, I tend to speed everywhere just to get it over with. Basically driving makes me feel like a hazard to myself and others. And of course there's the environmental thing. Global warming really scares me. I don't mind the bus. Too much."

She'd left a lot out, but her answer felt rambling already, so she stopped. She was thinking, though, of the times she *did* mind the bus, and, in spite of herself, of the people who rode it: ex-convicts and addicts in rehab; welfare recipients and visitors to free clinics. The bus *to* the small religious university was usually all right, but Martin tried to pick her up to take her home so she wouldn't have to make friends with late-night bus people.

When Martin was working a closing shift, Kathy would start class with the question, "Anybody going to Tacoma?" Mercifully, somebody usually would be, Brian or Allison most likely, non-traditional students living off campus. Brian, a communications major and Charlie's drinking buddy, liked to head down to T-town to visit his brother. Kathy liked sitting high in the passenger seat of his big red truck, listening to Brian talk about the day his luck had turned around, when he'd decided to stop being a drug-dealing fuckup and do something with his life. He was closer to her age than the other students, and easy to talk to. Kathy liked sitting low next to Allison in her father's tiny VW, the original key to which was missing, its gears jacked up, so it was loud on the highway, like being locked in a rock tumbler, all clattery-rumbly. Allison too was older, had gone to art school for a while, run away to Europe, and been in a destructive relationship. She was probably the best writer in the class—talented, dreamy, seemingly unaware of the full extent of her skills.

"I know what you mean," said Stevie, and for a second Kathy thought Stevie was going to cry. Stevie's last essay had been about her best friend from California who'd died, asleep at the wheel. But Stevie pulled it together and added, "I loved living in Manhattan, taking the subway everywhere."

"Yeah, exactly," said Kathy. "That's just one more reason I'm looking forward to Chicago. The El and all."

"I totally don't get it," said Charlie. "I love to drive. I bet you'll change your mind some day. You'll get a car and you'll see what I mean. All that power. All that speed."

He took the last drag, stubbed the butt on his boot and dropped it in the empty Blue Moon bottle Audrey'd set up as an ashtray.

Kathy had never gotten a ride with Charlie, a fact that now filled her with mild regret. She remembered one night, she'd been standing outside the small green house that contained her basement office, waiting for Martin to arrive in his sensible Ford Taurus, when Charlie'd sped by in his heart-red Mustang. It was twilight, surprisingly light out, and she was wearing a purple dress, winter-pale legs beneath the frothy dark skirt. Charlie had slowed down, top-down, had grinned and waved, his square hand shooting up like a periscope just behind the windshield, before speeding up again, motor whining, around the corner and out of sight. The gesture had struck her. It looked almost easy, but not quite—as if Charlie himself had hoped the action looked natural, but still wound up with something careful and practiced.

"Burgers are ready!" Audrey hollered from the kitchen in a cheerleader voice. They filed back inside.

After the frenzy of food-grabbing had subsided, Charlie and Kathy remained at the table among the condiments as Charlie doctored his fake burger, trying to make it look and taste more like meat.

"That's all you're eating? Seriously?" He set down the mustard and eyed her plate, which contained only the vegetarian bean salad she'd brought as her potluck contribution. Charlie's contribution had been the beer, of which they'd each had three.

"I'm not that hungry," she explained.

"So I thought your husband was going to be kind of a douche bag," said Charlie, taking a bite of his burger and chewing contemplatively.

"Why the hell would you think that?" she laughed.

"I guess it's more like I was hoping he'd be a douche bag," said Charlie. "So you might like me better."

"Too bad he's awesome," said Kathy.

"Yeah, too bad. He's really, really nice. And really tall."

Other students had had crushes on her in the past. In last semester's American Writers on War, for instance, one such student had pulled Kathy's shirt over her bra strap when she was sitting next to him, listening to a presentation. The young man had been, like many in that class, a member of the military, and it occurred to her later that he'd been trying to be chivalrous, to cover her up and see that she was decent. At the time, she'd been too surprised to say anything, had flinched. Another student from that class had asked her out to a concert. And there had been several others, girls and boys alike, mostly cute, mostly harmless. Charlie, though, was the most persistent. Charlie was the one she really liked.

When Kathy was nervous, which was often, she couldn't eat, but she sat on Audrey's couch and made herself tonight. The beers had gone to her head, and she didn't want to get drunk, fun as it had been when her own professors had done it. She liked to maintain—here, especially—an air of propriety. She was still the teacher. Martin never drank. She spied him across the room, chatting with Audrey and her roommate. As she ate a bite of salad, she felt a rush of affection for this class. They were not the privileged and unquestioning breed of student this small religious university seemed to pride itself on attracting, on coddling, on providing a safe home for.

From her vantage on the sofa, she looked at Chelsea, the transfer student with severe ADD who was late every single day, who'd moved with her strange and mysterious family over twenty-three times in her twenty-one years. Kathy looked at skinny, straight-haired, horse-loving Katie who was only in the class because of her best friend Bethany. She looked at Bethany, a former cutter, recovering from an eating disorder, and Celeste, the hairdresser, returned to college to complete her degree, and Joslin from Hawaii whose parents had split when she was ten and who wrote a wonderful piece about code-switching, swapping between Pidgin and the dialect of the mainland. She looked at Ryan, a sensitive kid whose dad was in the military, and at Beth, the third grade teacher, spacey and patient.

She loved this class, really loved them. She loved all her students, wanted to teach forever, but couldn't due to circumstance. Back in December, her boss had told her that no matter how good a job she did—and she was doing a good one—they just didn't know if they'd have the line of funding at this small university to keep her; she'd best start making other plans. So she had. But as attached as she had been to all her students, she felt fond of these ones in particular because they were difficult, complicated; were not guaranteed to love her back. Kathy liked a challenge. She liked things to *mean* something; she liked things to *matter*.

She set her half-empty plate down and wandered outside. Her students offered her a postprandial cigarette, and she accepted. It was another novelty kind: chocolate flavored. There were enough for each to have his or her own this time, all four of them: Audrey, Charlie, Stevie, and Kathy.

Higher than the sun now, which had sunk farther on the horizon but had not quite gone down, were the enormous planes, flying low over Parkland, lower over Spanaway, into and out of McChord Air Force Base. Roaring, large, and cylindrical, their wings jutted sharply and their engines were huge. Kathy had looked them up. They were C-17 Globemaster IIIs. They specialized in rapid strategic delivery of troops and cargo.

Martin worked at a major corporate bookstore in another sweetly named but sad suburb: Lakewood, rife with strip malls but lacking a lake and possessing only a few woods. Close to both McChord and Fort Lewis, Lakewood's town center, where the bookstore was located, was frequented by service people and their families. Martin had told Kathy that customers came in waves. Before a deployment, the aisles were flush with men in buzz cuts, women in fatigues. They would buy up paperbacks, light books that were thick but would travel well; fantasy and sci-fi were especially popular. After a deployment, the store would have the silence of a ghost town, the unreality of a soundstage. During those times, the occasional wives would come in, young but fading, harried with multiple children, usually all under ten, to send reading material to their husbands in Iraq.

The sun hit the wing of one of the planes, like the magnesium flash of an old-fashioned camera. Kathy blinked and as her eyes closed she saw the scene clearly—an old painters' trick: look at what's before you for a few seconds, then blink. Your mind will still see it, with even greater clarity, and it will help your composition. That was what happened. As her eyes were shut, she saw her students' faces, as yet unlined, their promise and pain.

Charlie looked at the plane and said, "I hate this state. I can't wait to leave. If I were my parents, living like they do, I'd have put a bullet in my brain twenty years ago."

Never mind that Charlie was only twenty-one, and that twenty years ago he'd been just an infant. Charlie had written about how he was a fraternal twin, the son of a steelworker who erected buildings in Seattle, where Charlie's twin brother Corey worked alongside him. Corey made lots of money and owned the house that he and Charlie lived in. Charlie had to pay rent to Corey, and Corey would yell at him when he played his guitar— his git-fiddle Charlie called it—too loud.

"My father is such a tightwad bastard. He has all this money, but he'll never spend any."

"What's he going to do with it?" asked Audrey.

"Die with it," said Charlie.

"I never really got to know my dad," said Audrey, who had written in an essay that her father had been a drug addict and had died when she was a baby.

Mount Rainier was not at the right angle for them to see it, but Kathy looked for it anyway. It was her favorite Washington sight. "I wish we could see the mountain from here. I read that if it erupted, it would bury Puyallup in an eleven-foot wave of boiling hot mud."

"Good riddance," Charlie said. "That's what I say." He began to giggle and then everyone did.

"I hate to say it, but I've gotta run. I've gotta go back to campus to catch my friend in *Cabaret*," said Stevie, her lanky arm reaching to put out her cigarette in the ashtray, mistaking Kathy's full bottle for the empty one, where it sizzled then floated atop the ruined beer.

"Oh shit, Stevie," said Audrey, realizing her mistake.

"Party foul, Stevie," Kathy teased, as Stevie looked mortified and blushed bright pink.

"Oh my god, I'm so sorry! I should have watched what I was doing," said Stevie.

"It's really okay," said Kathy, but Stevie insisted she take her full beer instead, as a replacement, since all the Blue Moons were gone. There were other beers in the fridge, but that was the best. To help Stevie feel better, Kathy accepted.

At some point, it got dark out and time began to telescope as it often did when Kathy had been drinking, when she was at a first-rate party. Everything began to happen quickly in disjointed fragments. *I am having fun*, she thought, looking at her watch, *and time is flying*.

The callbox buzzed in Audrey's living room; the nicotine buzzed in Kathy's brain.

Kathy and Martin stayed, and no one thought it unbecoming. Kathy had worried about lingering too late; it troubled her that she related better to her students than she did to most of her colleagues. To her knowledge, she was the only faculty member under thirty at her small religious university, since Chrissie had had her birthday back in January.

The night became a montage of going inside and coming back out, of questions and answers, of jokes and smokes, of trips to the bathroom and trips to the fridge.

"So where do you and Martin live?" Audrey was asking, tucking a glossy strand of blonde hair behind a triple-pierced ear. She was looking to move out of Parkland and into Tacoma, but she wanted to find a neighborhood that wasn't totally terrifying. Tacoma was up-and-coming, but it still had problems, meth and firearms.

"The TV show *Cops* gets filmed in Tacoma quite a bit," the sweet departmental assistant had told Kathy on the phone the previous August, while she and Martin were looking online for apartments. "There are a lot of places with pretty names—Lakewood, Parkland, but they're not really so nice."

One of her colleagues, the department's fiction writer, had offered to help her decide where to look. Every time she sent him the listing of a place that looked perfect in the picture and cost a reasonable price, he'd write back in the negative. "Nope," again and again. "Gun nuts," he'd written, and "Pitbulls," and "Chainlink fences." "Okay," she'd written back. "Okay, okay," and then she'd start over.

She and Martin finally ended up in the historic North Slope near the Stadium District, both of which were areas she recommended to Audrey.

"We live in a building called The Biltmore with these huge marble griffins in front," Kathy said. "It's up the street from the mayor's old mansion. Obviously, there's going to be a vacancy soon."

"Wow, that sounds classy," said Audrey.

Kathy agreed that yes, it was classy, but classy in the way a Gothic-font tattoo of someone's name was classy—the faux-British title and the white stone creatures, feathered wings streaming and carved tongues sticking out in obscene KISS faces. Still though, Kathy was going to miss the place.

Then they were asking her why she was leaving, didn't she love teaching? And she was explaining that yes, she loved it, but that was the way things sometimes worked in the academy.

Then Kathy was lighting her cigarette inexpertly, the lighter flame guttering in the high dry wind, more characteristic of late summer than spring. She was about to give up when Charlie leaned in and said, "Here, light off mine."

Kathy's lips were inches from Charlie's, her eyes locked on the cigarette, making sure to keep it even, his eyes locked on her lips, her face, her eyes.

"Butt sex!" Joslin cried out gleefully.

"You are fulfilling," Audrey said, "one of Charlie's wildest dreams."

She pulled away, took a drag, and Charlie sighed.

Martin stayed inside most of the night between the kitchen and the picked-over food table stripped bare of Boca burgers, talking to one of Audrey's erstwhile flings, a business major, and apparently a good conversationalist.

Then someone brought out a bunny—of course, a bunny, why not?—Audrey's pet rabbit. His name was Seymour.

Then Audrey and her roommate were demonstrating "wining," a grinding, ass-centric style of dance Audrey had learned studying abroad in Trinidad and Tobago.

"Need a big bootied woman for me to wine up on," said the stereo. Next she did the routine of a Trini boy band she'd hung out with on the islands.

Charlie, meanwhile, had been waylaid on his way back from the bathroom—very drunk now, and teetering slightly—and was trying to convince Martin to buy a fast car, to be in a band. He was not too drunk, though, to reach into the vice box for the hot pink deck and to perform for them a trick, a rather complicated one, a story really. It was a fairytale complete with kings, queens, princes, and princesses, and the plot had to do with everyone ending up, against all odds, as part of a rightful couple with their proper partner.

Kathy wondered where he'd be in another ten years; wondered what he'd be like. She wondered where she'd be in another ten years and what she'd be like as well.

Then Audrey was showing her scrapbooks to Kathy, seated next to her on the blue velour couch: concerts and recitals and her heroic single mother, whom Audrey clearly revered.

Kathy was promising Audrey that yes, of course, she'd help Audrey get into art modeling, one of the jobs Kathy did on the side in Tacoma.

"So where can I go to see some of those pictures of you, Kathy?" Charlie was asking.

"In your dreams, Charlie, in your dreams."

Charlie kept calling Martin her boyfriend. Kathy kept correcting him at first, and then gave up.

Then Brian was telling Kathy and Joslin about the time he got jumped on his way home from a party by some guys he knew from his dealing days. He'd gotten a concussion and still had issues with his short-term memory.

Then Brian was telling her about a French teacher there at the small religious university who'd had an affair with one of her students. The French teacher was in her early thirties, Kathy's friend and sometime yoga buddy, a person to whom she would have liked to get closer, but who was something of a homebody with a younger husband who hardly spoke English and seemed kind of gay.

Who knew if what Brian was saying was true? "What was the student's name?" asked Kathy. "Graham something," said Brian, with Joslin corroborating, but Kathy did not know him, did not recognize the last name and so forgot it immediately.

Kathy thought about the possible logistics of such a liaison. She remembered being alone with Charlie in her office, when he was attending the appointment she made all of them keep, believing it was important that she talk to each of them about their writing one on one, face to face. She was explaining to him how to motivate his writing, how to make each sentence, each word, serve a definite purpose, and he was looking sometimes at the paper she had marked up so much it seemed to be dipped in pink ink, but mostly he looked at the side of her face. He smelled nice, she remembered, smoky but nice. She wished he didn't smoke as much. She wanted him not to age, not to die, to stay this way forever. For herself too, she wanted this; she wanted this for all of them. But it was a stupid, impossible, foolish wish. Kathy was full of them.

Charlie was looking at the side of her face now, and asking her another question, "How many beers have you had? You don't even seem drunk yet."

"Well, I'm not drunk yet. Do I seem drunk to you?" she asked Brian and Joslin, who laughed.

"I don't know about that," Brian replied. "But if you have to ask, then you're probably not sober."

"Excellent point," she said, admiring his logic.

Then Audrey was reaching behind Kathy to plug in the dragonfly lights. "I got these at Target. I've been dying to use them."

"So Kathleen, tell me," Charlie was saying, drunker now and calling her by her full first name. "How many?" He wanted to know how many men she'd slept with.

"None of your damn business," she said. "How many for you?"

"Thirteen," he said. "Women, I mean."

"Lucky number thirteen," said Kathy-Kathleen, doubting, but impressed. Wondering if it could be true, and guessing yes.

Then someone had brought out a pair of bunny-fur earmuffs.

"They were a gift," Audrey, a member of PETA, explained.

These were put on Brian, and a knit cap was put on Charlie, aqua blue and retro, a winning color combination with his shiny brown hair.

Then Kirsten brought out a lambskin hat, fluffy as a cloud, as a dandelion, as a cotton ball, as—a lamb.

"You get to wear this one," Kirsten said, and handed it to Kathy, who normally disliked hats, but who put it on anyway. It seemed like the polite thing to do.

Her husband said the hat recalled the late '50s photograph of the actress Tuesday Weld on the cover of Matthew Sweet's pop album *Girlfriend*, though Kathy was not blonde, not in the '50s, and not anyone's girlfriend.

"You look fabulous in that," said Kirsten, snapping her photograph.

"You look fabulous in anything," said Joslin.

Audrey agreed and Kathy wanted to correct them, wondered how such smart young people could be so wrong.

"Did you read the portfolios yet?" Charlie asked.

"No," Kathy lied. "I haven't had time. But I will. I'm looking forward to it. I read all the letters really carefully."

Brian shot a meaningful look at Charlie, and Joslin snickered.

"What's so funny? I'm probably going to read them tomorrow. Charlie, did you write something mean? What did you write?"

"Nothing," Charlie sighed. "Never mind."

There were many things that Kathy was going to do tomorrow, but grading the portfolios was not one of them, since they were already done. She would teach her last 101 class, and she would go to another party, another barbecue, this one at the Faculty House, the members-only club for employees.

This barbecue would be geriatric in comparison, full of sober oldsters. The weather that day would be gray and noncommittal and would remind her again why she was happy to be leaving. Academia as represented by this small religious university had felt to her a bit like prison. A really luxurious white-collar prison, but still a prison insofar as it had always felt too small, too confined, and too homogenous.

Most people at this barbecue wouldn't know her, wouldn't remember her name, though she'd been there a year. The few who did, who knew she was leaving, would ask her again, though she'd told them before, where she was going, what she was up to next, and she would get sick of replying. Her veggie burger would lay half-eaten on her plate and she would get up and dump it in the trash.

She would need to get away from it all: the aluminum siding, the nametags. The barbecue grill with the bartender from the basement upstairs now, in the yard, middle-aged and balding, clowning with a huge obscene hot dog in his mouth. The mothball-smelling fellowship, the stale leaves in the gutters, and the musty Christianity.

She would wander into a back room and sit, legs propped up on the gray faux leather sofa, waiting to be found, but nobody would find her. She would wonder if she hated the place so much because she feared it, feared becoming it, feared becoming like them, but wondering wouldn't stop the hate. She would want to scream, to cry, to run as far away as her brown ballet flats would take her. Instead, she would say, "Hey Chrissie, let's blow this popsicle stand," and they would round up their younger friends and beg them to leave, and that's what they would do.

A sign on Audrey's freezer said I ♥ ANTHONY HOPKINS beneath a crinkly photocopy of a black-and-white photograph of the actor, back when he'd been young.

Then Kathy was staring into the glowing fridge, lined with beers, rigid and neat on the top two shelves and on the lowest ones, sodas Audrey had stolen one at a time from her job. Kathy was thinking about the pleasure and the thrill of flattery, of knowing you could be very bad if you wanted to, that there was someone out there willing to get together and be bad with you who would, at the drop of a curious fuzzy hat, drop everything, say, to make out with you in the bathroom. And it occurred to her, gazing into the cold white purity of the fridge, that there were lots of things she could do, but that she shouldn't— and therefore wouldn't—do them. And this felt good: power and responsibility.

Then it was one in the morning and Kathy and Martin were leaving. A few students were still staying.

"Don't go," Charlie was saying, said again, kept saying.

But she had to go and so she went, not without sadness, and not without regret. She did not want to be the last to leave the party, literally or metaphorically, and she tried to tell herself that she was glad to be leaving. There was no more progress to be made. They liked her so much and she liked them, but better to leave on top of your game than old and injured and not to be missed. Still she despised this, the awkwardness of good-byes. She was hugging everyone, even the kid not in her class, the business major with a vocation in coaching who'd been chatting with Martin all evening.

"Stay a little longer?" Charlie said, his brown eyes pleading, a practiced puppy-dog look.

"You shouldn't act so adult now," Paul Westerberg yowled like a tomcat from the stereo, full of ridiculous and impossible longing.

"Sorry, Charlie," she said. "But this is good-bye. You're a really good writer; please don't stop."

He hugged her, let go, then hugged her one more time.

Then she and Martin were descending the stairs, heading to the Taurus, parked next to Charlie's red Mustang. Charlie would not, thankfully, be driving home that night. Martin pointed out that maybe Audrey threw the barbecue in the first place to get Charlie into bed. And Kathy thought maybe he was right, but not entirely. That might have been part of the reason, maybe, but Audrey liked to host, Audrey liked Kathy. And sure, maybe she liked Charlie, but she was a complicated girl. Audrey was, after all, a known cheater, and she had already had several angry phone conversations that night with her boyfriend back in her small hometown. And it made Kathy sad, the thought that perhaps Charlie was not just going to stay *at* Audrey's, but *with* her, that the blue velour couch might not be where he slept, but rather Audrey's bed.

Charlie had spoken once in class of what he and his friends called the DDF: Distance Distortion Factor.

"It's when a girl looks hot from far away, but when you get closer, something's askew. A feature's wrong or a few are, and the whole effect is ruined," he'd explained.

"It happens on guys too," he'd added hastily, when she'd leveled him with a look and raised an eyebrow. She'd been working all semester on getting him to be just a little more evolved in his gender attitudes.

Kathy would think, at that faculty barbecue of the living dead, that the DDF could occur with places, with institutions too. That maybe that's what had happened with the small religious university. It had looked so perfect at first from so far away, over three thousand miles and a dozen states, but shortly after she'd actually arrived and seen it with her own eyes, the flaws became obvious: its tiny size, barely bigger than the high school she'd gone to, its God squad façade belying its ruthless interior, and the way that a great deal of what had been promised—the opening of a tenure track position, the option to stay on—had been misrepresentations, if not outright lies.

As Martin was driving them home from Audrey's, back to T-town, among the semis on the 705, the party at Audrey's was already becoming a memory. Kathy was already having nostalgia about that time, that one time, there on Audrey's balcony when she took one final drag from her last cigarette, a regular one, a Basic she'd drawn from Charlie's pack, turning one upside down as she did before handing it back.

"For luck," she'd explained.

She'd exhaled over the railing, above the twinkling dragonflies, watching the smoke curl up and away into the sky where she could see a few stars, and more clearly, signals from the low-flying planes going about their military-industrial business even this late, even past midnight. Softened by alcohol and mellowed by haze with their red and white flares flashing brightly in the darkness, even the planes looked pretty, inviting. Even they looked like something good, like something worthwhile was happening here, in this time, in this place.

FIRST PERSON
IMPOSSIBLE

I had a most marvelous piece of luck. I died.

—JOHN BERRYMAN, "DREAM SONG 26"

*T*HIS IS a ghost story. I am one of the ghosts.
Ghosts experience boundaries differently than most.

Smells are ghostly, as is light. Sounds are ghostly, radio waves too.

Time is ghostly and especially time zones.

Ghost stories are really just stories about history.

My husband and I are driving a sixteen-foot Budget truck through "The American West" to head East. Rather, he is driving and I am riding shotgun.

In Washington state, we pass Kent, its logging rampant: stumps and trunks and stacks of single logs spread brown on the green green ground, as if someone had dipped her fingertips in a box of toothpicks, hoisted and then let them fall where they would—inscrutable configurations. If I looked long enough, they might spell out words.

My husband is driving because I do not drive. Vehicles to me seem like rolling coffins; all that motion, that potential for death.

We are crossing borders, like ghosts through walls. We are crossing state lines and the Continental Divide.

The arc of this story is natural; it has both a start- and an endpoint: Tacoma to Chicago, point A to point Z and some stops in between, the extent of the alphabet we need to cross, seven large states in three or so days.

Two of my students are driving our car. I am already becoming a ghost to them. A fuzzy pleasant part of a pleasant fuzzy time. The person from whom they learned autobiographical writing. They are driving my auto, part of my biography.
School has been out for half a month, and already I am becoming a person in their memory, a face they'll think back on and say, "Remember when, in Rooney's class, that one time . . . ?" That is, if I'm lucky. Some of them might some day not recall me at all.

A "normal" couple might have one spouse drive the moving van and the other drive the Ford Taurus, but I suppose we are not a "normal" couple, or else I am not a "normal" wife.

Other professors at the small religious university I am leaving—many of whom seemed to wish I was a ghost to them already—had wrung their hands at the students-driving plan. What if something happened to them, to the students, to Michael and Vy? Oh, the liability!

Some of them smiled tight little smiles and praised my bravery, in this case, a polite synonym for "foolishness" or "stupidity," much like "ambition" is a euphemism for people you think try hard, but aren't naturally great.

Ghosts have nothing to lose. They are already dead. You can't take their lives so what can you take?

I have already lost my job. "What are they gonna do—fire me?" has been my mantra since December when my boss came into my office at the small religious university and gently suggested I "make other plans."

My belief that hard work and talent eventually receive their due is becoming more ghostly.

Michael and Vy have never been East, and they are very excited, even though we are only ending up in the Midwest.

I am supposed to be reading a contemporary fiction writer to prepare for an interview. Instead I can't stop reading John Berryman, a non-contemporary poet, though I've read him before and he is long since dead; I'll never interview him.

My neglectfulness won't matter, I reason, if we crash along the way, so I might as well go on reading whatever makes me happy.

"As a kid I believed in democracy," Berryman writes. I still do, though I am not a kid. That's why I'm headed where I'm headed, to the heart of the heartland, to be a Chicago-based campaign worker for the Democratic Party.

At the end of the road, I'll return, for a month or so, to my parents' house, my childhood home, the site of my adolescence. I will sleep with my husband in the bedroom I haven't occupied permanently since I was eighteen. I will be doing so at a time in my life when society tells me I really should be more rooted, more stable, more adult.

"By most accounts . . . Berryman never quite evolved into a sane, stable adult. Gangly, often-bearded, Berryman was an insomniac, a hypochondriac, an accident-prone, chain-smoking alcoholic and a depressive with suicidal tendencies, inept at carrying out daily tasks like cooking or driving a car." I love to cook, but driving evades me. I used to try, vaguely, to overcome my aversion, but I've since given up and the longer it goes on, the less it seems like a phase and the more it becomes an enduring (endearing?) quirk. I live on foot, close to the ground, walking around my cities and towns, except when I'm up, like here, like now in our sixteen-foot Budget truck.

My students are lower down and I don't know which one is at the wheel at the moment, Michael or Vy. They left a day after us and are taking I-90, to the south, whereas we're on I-94, veering north to swing through Minneapolis, former home of the poet

John Berryman, current home of two recently married friends from grad school in Boston.

When we woke up this morning, Martin and I were in Spokane. It was raining, hard, and it continued to rain all the way through Idaho, Coeur d'Alene and onward.

"The horizon is all cloud," Berryman writes in *The Dream Songs* whose pages I flip, sometimes so quickly they sound like rain. "Leaves on leaves on leaves of books I've turned / and I know nothing."

It is summer now, early June, but the weather on this drive has been fearsome, cold and windy with driving rain. My job, as the non-driver, is to navigate and work the radio. But since our directions consist of (1) get on the highway, and (2) head straight east, I focus my attention on scanning through stations, trying to avoid listening to (1) country, or (2) religion. Frequently, the thing to do is just settle on oldies.

Sometimes, the rain gets so heavy, we can't hear anything anyway. Sometimes the clouds break. Then the backup singers say: "sockittomesockittomesockittomesockittomesockittomesockittomesockittomesockittome," and the weather does.

Michael and Vy are to call every night at 9:00 when minutes become free, and to keep all their receipts. We've already paid them—gas, food, lodging, and two plane tickets home—but we have impressed upon them the importance of the tax write-off.

Before we'd all set out, they'd shown me the binder they'd created, special for this occasion, recycled from the final port-folios they'd had to turn in for my class: directions from both MapQuest and Google Maps, tourist information on the major attractions and sights along the way, places to eat in Bozeman, Montana, where they would stop the first night, and details about the Corn Palace in Mitchell, South Dakota, where they would stay the second, as well as CTA bus and El schedules for the Windy City.

When Vy showed up to class each day with her color-coded notebooks and alphabetized folders, I always got the urge to hire her for something, anything, because whatever the situation, she gave the impression of having it well in hand. The daughter of Vietnamese immigrants, she'd emancipated herself from her mother and stepdad at the age of fourteen. She had the maturity you'd expect in a person who could pull off that kind of thing.

Michael was tall and blond with a widow's peak, a former aficionado of vampire fiction whom none of the other creative writing professors would allow in their already full classes. I over-enrolled mine to let him in, to help him get the credits he needed for his English major. He'd turned out to be well read and a strong writer, at least autobiographically. It's hard to write about Dracula, I guess, when it's your own life in question.

Leaving Missoula after stopping for lunch on the second day, Martin barrels the sixteen-foot Budget truck through a stale yel-low light. I kiss my fingertips with a smack and slap the ceiling. My husband's a champion driver, but I can be superstitious. Oddly, I'm not worried about Michael and Vy; I trust them completely.

A friend of mine, an adjunct professor in Boston, sent me an email recently, after I'd written about how much I disliked the small religious university, even though I loved my students. "What fascinates me is how you blur that student-teacher line," she wrote. "Perhaps it's a bias as I'm someone who never partied with my undergrad professors."

Berryman was not what you'd call a nice guy, but apparently he was charming and a genius besides. Berryman won the National Book Award and the Pulitzer Prize. Berryman was known to party with his students.

At the Iowa Writers' Workshop, when Berryman was on the faculty, "Phil Levine punched Berryman in the eye one night, breaking a pair of glasses and establishing a life-long friendship. These kinds of personal relationships were important to Berryman. It is a question of whether he influenced his students more than they influenced him."

I wrote my friend back, "I tend to have a hard time being strictly 'professional.' I guess, if people reach out to me in a human/friendly way, I tend to weigh the possibilities and then reach back."

The woman who mentored us in grad school warned us within the first five minutes of the new teacher orientation: "If you see your students at a bar, run the other way."

Michael, Vy, Martin, and I arranged to meet for drinks at a bar near the small religious university a few days before the big drive. I did not run when Michael emailed to invite us, and when I arrived, I suggested a pitcher.

I treat my students like adults because that is what they are, or at least that is what we are all supposed to be.

In Washington and Montana, we pass truckloads and truckloads of plastic-covered parts labeled KUWAIT STRYKERS in bold block letters. After we arrive in Illinois, I will look up what that means and learn that Strykers are a family of eight-wheel-drive combat vehicles, built for the U.S. Army by General Dynamics Land Systems of Canada. This will make sense, to the extent that war machines can make any sense: the fact that we were seeing so many so far north, close to the border, between all the military bases. We pass by several in Western Washington, and one in Minot, North Dakota, a town which seems to exist for no reason other than to maintain its Air Force base.

"The war is real," Berryman writes. "And a sullen glory pauses over them harmed, / incident to murder." Sullen, certainly; glorious, not this way, on that flatbed, in this rain.

Because of the weather, everything begins to feel increasingly dreamlike—gray road, gray sky, a perpetual twilight. I am happy to be leaving, excited even, but melancholy over the reasons. So much of this past year has felt like a dream, not just surreal, but like an actively bad dream.

"I can't go into the meaning of the dream / except to say a sense of total loss / afflicted me thereof," writes Berryman. "An absolute disappearance of continuity and love / and children away at school, the weight of the cross, / and everything is what it seems."

I move around like someone who will never be satisfied. I have moved eleven times in the nine years since I left my childhood home.

Many cultures have a concept called the Hungry Ghost, the ghost who doesn't even know she is one, who spent her life in pursuit of worldly satisfactions, who died, and who still has cravings. She is said to have a stomach the size of a mountain and a mouth the size of a pin.

Berryman denied that Henry in *The Dream Songs* was his alter ego, even though he was—his shadow, his shade. Even though Berryman was a Confessional Poet. Even though his work was autobiographical. He was hardly ever happy. He was hardly ever satisfied.

In Eastern Montana, in a break in the rain, Martin and I stop for a snapshot at Pompey's Pillar. It is named for the son of Sacagawea. His real name was Jean-Baptiste, but Clark of Lewis-and- decided he should be known as Pompey, Pomp for short, so that is what this chimney of striated rock—colorful, layered like Neapolitan ice cream—gets called. Clark carved his name and the year into the base of the stone. Clark acted like a teen. What do I mean by that and what does that mean?

The rain starts up again. I am being morbid and the sky is gelid. No telling how long this storm will last. The sixteen-foot Budget truck shakes and shudders in the wind. Martin's face remains stoic, though he likens the conditions to "trying to walk down the street during a gale carrying a dry erase board—it feels like a sail." At least our truck is full, freighty. The trailer in front of us is empty, fishtailing south as the wind blasts from the north. There were not many to begin with, but people are starting to pull off the interstate. We hate to keep driving, but there's nowhere else to go.

The Christian mystic Emanuel Swedenborg said sometimes the dead don't even know they're the dead; they just go on doing whatever it is they'd set out to do in life. Alone, out here in the dying light, I say, "Maybe that's us," and Martin laughs. There's nobody ahead, nobody heading west, nobody in the rearview. "Maybe we'll drive like this forever," he says.

I find a station that sounds like magic. In a stroke of insight, driven by desperation—*please no more country, no more god squad radio*—I switch to AM: K-something 1250 out of Miles City and Forsyth. AM stations are tinny, not in stereo, and they echo like a voice across the bottom of a canyon.

The DJ remains nameless, an indistinct figure behind the creaky music, playing songs from the '40s and '50s that pipe into the cab of our sixteen-foot Budget truck like the contents of a time capsule. He tosses in a couple by ABBA, one by Debbie Gibson, but nothing more recent than that before it's back to obscure Elvis: that buttery voice, those spangled backup singers hooting like owls. The DJ never plays the hits, just the lesser knowns and the effect is uncanny, the sonic personification of Freud's *unheimlich*.

It feels like we are listening to a soundtrack on eight-track. "If there were a number," I say, "I'd call it just to tell that guy hi and thanks."

Oneiromancy is the art of divination through dreams. Radiomancy would be the art of divination through the radio. Maybe if we called and got a hold of the guy, he could listen to our voices and look into our futures and communicate them to us through the medium of song. But there never is any number and there are hardly any call letter announcements, and the only indication that this isn't some endlessly looped pre-recorded tape playing from somebody's basement—that any of this is real or earthly—is when the program gets interrupted by that high-pitched emergency tone and that honky-skronky goose sound telling us that the weather is bad. "We know," we laugh. "We know." Then, the man's voice, crackly with static and broken by lightning, says, "A flash flood warning is in effect . . . three inches of rain in under an hour . . . Forsyth and Miles City . . . all of Custer County . . . advised to seek shelter . . ."

"These lovely motions of the air, the breeze," writes Berryman, "tell me I'm not in hell, though round me the dead / lie in their limp postures / dramatizing the dreadful word *instead*."

Instead of our original plan—dinner at a cowboy bar in downtown Miles City—we try to make for high ground, getting to the outskirts just as the water is beginning to encroach seriously, creeping to the shoulder and over the highway.

I am freaked out, skittish as a colt, but the few patrons in the Pizza Hut near our motel where we place our To Go order are calm, bovine, ruminating over the salad bar like cows with cud. The Motel 6 clerk, when I ask her if this torrent's normal, says yes, it is, a typical spring, but it's been so long since they've had one that they don't quite know what to do with it.

We settle into our room just as my cellphone rings, Michael and Vy, safe in Bozeman, all in one piece. Then the TV show we are watching turns to salad, raggedy patches of jagged color, then snaps out completely as the lights go dark—nothing to do now but go to bed. The rain stops around midnight, but the wind keeps howling like a wolf for hours, waking me as it blows the curtains back into the room, though the windows are closed. I ask Martin if we'll be safe and he murmurs that a tornado sounds like a freight train not a wolf, now go back to sleep.

"Them lady poets must not marry, pal," Berryman writes, and, "It is a true error to marry with poets / or to be by them."

The next morning is full of pleas, billboarded from the road-side, trying to sound fun, but coming across as needy: Historic Forts, Water Parks, and Dinosaur Fossils. The signs that say things like, "Visit White Cloud, the Albino Buffalo, Jamestown, ND," but sound like, "Stop, stop, stop c'mon, please, and see us" but we don't. We keep going, and it keeps on raining, the wind whipping white caps on the man-made lakes.

At Dickinson, we finally lose our AM station. I find some standard-issue oldies just as we pull off an exit just past the North Dakota border for some overpriced gas.

"What ever happened to Political Economy, / leaving me here?" writes Berryman. "The military establishments perpetuate themselves forever. / Have a bite, for a sign."

We pull under the gas station overhang with its dripping beams and fluorescent lights as Janis Joplin is squalling, "O, Lord, won't you buy me a color TV . . ." Martin pumps and our sixteen-foot Budget truck guzzles. From my seat, I see we are in a land of people who look like they still watch black-and-white, everyone old and going nowhere.

Almost everything we pass professes to be the World's Largest. In a place so small-time but with so much space, the only way to assert one's importance appears to be through sheer colossal size. We see signs for The World's Largest Metal Sculptures, which we would actually really like to stop and see if the weather weren't so crappy. The only one we can view from the road? A huge human eye, watching geese fly in their traditional V across its iris—but wait, surprise! The geese are *part of* the eye, a connection, a blurring, an absence of boundaries, haunting and ghostly. It looks like those craft projects people used to make in the '70s, using black-felted particleboard with nails pounded in and thread-gauge copper wire, only this one is massive.

My father will tell us when we arrive that he's just read about the sculpture guy in *National Geographic*, but he hasn't saved the magazine. The sculptor is a retired schoolteacher who's just bought a farm, converting the barn into a workshop for his outsized creations. This is all just outside the South Unit of Theodore

Roosevelt National Park. T.R. had liked the place because it was so *big,* so empty.

When we stop in Jamestown in the middle of the state for some gas and sandwiches, it seems that all the residents are either in late middle-age at least, or mentally handicapped, or both. We think maybe we are dreaming, because how could that be? As we drive out the other side, we see how: the green-and-white sign for The Jamestown State Hospital. Martin laughs and cracks an inappropriate joke that involves the phrase "'Tard Farm." I laugh too, harder than I have in the three days since we left, and even as I do, I hope that God, in whom I don't even know if I believe, doesn't strike us both retarded for our terrible lack of charity. We are punchy from the road. We are seeing and saying things that we wouldn't normally. These people can't help being stuck where they are, can they? These people have souls.

"My air is flung with souls which will not stop / and among them hangs a soul that has not died / and refuses to come home."

We cross another time zone. Now we've lost two hours. Where did they go?

The weather makes one last brutal assault, a wall of water and tree branches everywhere. Again, people are pulling over, hunkering beneath overpasses. We are afraid of hail, and tornados maybe, but again we keep going—it's not our truck and we paid for the insurance.

We make it, finally, hurling ourselves against the door of Matt and Jana's suburban rambler, just as the wind dies down and the sun comes out.

"Heaven is here / now, in Minneapolis," Berryman writes, and it feels so good to be out of the truck, in the Midwest, among friends, that I have to agree.

Matt and Jana's power is out, but it is still daylight and everyone is so happy to see everyone else. Matt and Jana live in the suburbs now too, but it is not temporary; they are living by themselves, not with their parents like I soon will be. Minnesota is the Land of Ten Thousand Lakes and there is one in their neighborhood, a neighborhood full of refugees—people from Africa, and Hmong people from Asia who fish all day in the lake. "Are there fish in there?" I ask. "I hope so," says Matt. "For their sake."

Matt and Jana take us to the Walker Art Center and over a bridge with a John Ashbery poem printed on either side, a poem that is pretty and makes, characteristically, very little sense, a poem that ends, "And then it got very cool."

Every time I cross a bridge, I think about jumping. Is everyone like this?

We eat on top of a restaurant with a roof deck in the setting sun and the rising wind with a view of the basilica. The ghost of snow haunts Minneapolis-St. Paul, a cold white presence even in June. The streets are bare except for cars and branches, but I can see the snow, not just imagine it; see the outlines where it could

be pasted in, like a sticker in a book. The summer has a temporary mood and people drink it in like alcoholics with final drinks,
like determined quitters with last cigarettes. I picture the streets
with the snow piled up like tickertape, like feathers, like shredded
documents.

It is Matt's birthday. He is turning thirty-two. He and Jana
got married last week. Because it is Matt's birthday, we want to
go eat cake in St. Paul. We take the Washington Avenue Bridge
to get there, a bridge that is mostly covered, for the sake of the
students crossing back and forth between the sides of the campus
of the University of Minnesota in winter. This is the bridge that
John Berryman jumped from, waving to onlookers before throwing himself over one cold morning in January 1972. What is a
suicide? A question mark, maybe?

"It's really high," says Matt, whose own brother killed himself. "Death almost on impact. Almost instant probably."

I've read that a fall from such a great height negates the need
for water; you don't need to drown. The crash scrambles your or-
gans like eggs, which is good, if you can say that, because Berryman
had missed what he had been aiming for—the Mississippi River—
and crashed into the bank on the Minneapolis side.

"So now his thought's gone, buried his body dead," Berryman
writes, "will they set up a tumult in his praise / will assistant professors become associates by working on his works?"

Did Berryman have his notebook with him when he jumped?
Did it fly down next to him like a dove, a spirit, a holy ghost? He
professed Catholicism near the end of his life.

The cake is delicious. We go back to Matt and Jana's satisfied and sleep a better sleep than we have in nights.

The next day dawns sunny and bright and we eat our breakfasts and say our good-byes. Soon I-90 and I-94 run back into each other and I wonder, *Where are my students?* I could call them and find out, but I don't. I am caring, sure, but I am not the boss of them. I am not their mom. My students, it occurs to me, are not really my students anymore. I revise the thought, *Where are Michael and Vy?*

Two hundred miles from Chicago, the sights we see start to seem familiar: Black Cat Fireworks Stands, German Haus restaurants, and signs for the Wisconsin Dells and House on the Rock. The only place I'd want to stop that I went to as a kid—the Wonder Spot, where you can't stand straight and water flows up hill—just closed forever. My mom sent me a clipping. I picture throwing myself from the present into the past, colliding back into my former selves like a pack of cards reassembling into a deck. Like the erstwhile me's might still be ghosts, haunting the places I used to be.

My sister, Beth, calls to say how excited she is that I'm back again in the Central time zone. When Martin and I get an apartment in August, she wants it to be by her and her husband Nick's place on the north side of the city; we want that too.

"Watch out when you get home," she says. "It's the seventeen-year cicadas! Dad thought there weren't as many of them in Woodridge as there were in Downers Grove, so we smuggled some back. Now, every time we hear them, he asks 'Do you think those might be some of our little guys?'" She laughs.

As she tells me the story, I picture her and my dad at her in-laws' house, coveting the cicadas, longing to be lulled by their songs in the heat of the day and the cool of the night, gathering up five hundred or so of the bugs with wide-set eyes and veiny wings to put on the trees of our leafy green suburb. Cicadas are harmless. They are sometimes called locusts, but they are not the same thing. They do not eat crops, nor bite, nor sting.

When we finally arrive, Martin and I hear the cicadas, languid and dreamy, an eerie sawing from above, ahead, all sides and behind, like Sensurround.

"A good drone musician would aspire to make a sound like that, so harmonically dense," Martin says. "A song made up of tiny discrete units, individual clicks coming together in one beat-filled sound."

"They do it for love, and they don't live long," I say. "It's a mating song first, then a courtship song."

"That is our 'pointed task. Love & die," writes Berryman.

Michael and Vy arrive later that evening, and it occurs to me why some of my coworkers might have found my plan distasteful, unworkable for them personally, aside from the liability. I am letting my former students stay for the night with us in my parents' house. That's a lot of transparency; there's a risk there that they might see a lot of my ghosts.

I invite Michael and Vy to check their email on the computer in the basement, and Vy sees an old photograph my mother keeps near the desk: me from a long time ago, me in high school, me with my dark hair cut very, very short.

"You look darling in that style," says Vy, and Michael agrees, though I beg to differ. "How old were you?"

"How old was I?" I repeat. "I was seventeen. Yeah, about seventeen."

"Cute!" they say in unison.

I was ten years old when I saw my first seventeen-year cicadas. Where have the cicadas been and where have I? The cicadas look exactly the same as I remember them, but I have changed.

A friend I hadn't seen in ages saw a picture of me online and wrote to me how nice I look now with long hair, though I've had it for a while. "It's funny how people get frozen in your brain looking a certain way, the way they used to look when you saw them often," I wrote her back. You don't see them for real anymore and if they show up, it's only in your dreams and there they have their old hair, old clothes, old habits. They look like friendly ghosts.

My mom and dad feed us pizza and salad. Then Martin and I take Michael and Vy to a used bookstore to buy books for their return trip, a standby flight. It's Friday and they are leaving Sunday night. When we get back to my parents' house, we all eat the cake my mother made for the occasion: lemon pound in a Bundt pan—yellow, moist, and perfectly sugared. This is my idyllic Midwestern life. This is the love and feeding from which I originate. How does it look to outside eyes? How does it look to mine, away for so long?

This summer, the cicadas leave husky shells of themselves behind, golden and molty, crispy little ghosts. Kind of beautiful, kind of gross. I like to think of all kinds of ghosts as pretty. Gauzy. Filigreed. Like they're always seen from behind a lace curtain, with a vague sense of motion, white and clean.

ALWAYS
CRASHING
IN THE
SAME CAR

JUNE 21, 2007:
VOLKSWAGEN CABRIOLET, FOREST-GREEN

My boss, the chief of staff, pulls out of his reserved parking space in the basement of the federal building, and floors it as we hit the ramp that carries us up to street level. My head snaps back and bobbles a little like a figurine on a dash.

"You look smashing," he grins, as the sun from the west hits my face and we make our way toward Lake Shore Drive. "You should wear that all the time."

Patsy Cline is on the stereo, and I am wearing huge dark sunglasses and a hat he tossed me, as he put the top down, to keep my hair from getting tangled in the wind. I look disguised.

"And you should keep your eyes on the road," I say, and he's going to crack back, but then he's howling about being in the wrong lane, and I'm telling him he drives like Mr. Toad's Wild Ride.

We are on our way to an evening reception for the recently elected Water Commissioner. It's on the north branch of the Chicago River, on the waterfront green space behind—as the invitation puts it—"Chicago's newest, most modern, and stylish dog hotel." The lake is a scintillating blue to our right, and birds stir the sky, and we are surrounded by the hum of hundreds of engines as he weaves in and out of traffic like an ambulance driver, tapping the horn and swearing creatively: "Dickshit" he says, and "Dickoff," and "Fuckweed." I admire his innovation and remark that I'll have to remember them and try them out someday.

"Someday may be sooner than you think, babe," he replies.

"What do you mean?" I say, though I know the answer.

Our office has a driving pool. Every six to eight weeks, depending how we're staffed, the scheduler calls us to the conference room in our thirty-eighth-floor suite to pull numbers from a flame-red firefighter's hat. We then use those numbers to pick—one goes first, eight goes last—driving weeks, which is to say, the weeks that each of us will be charged with the patriotic responsibility of driving the senior senator from Illinois to and from all of his official engagements. There's money in the budget to hire a full-time driver, and I'm told that most senators do, but he is not most senators. He wants to get to know his staff, and one of the best ways to do that—as he learned from his mentor, a bow-tied senator—is to ride shotgun as they ferry him through the city, the suburbs, the state.

My coworker Sofia has already told me half a dozen times not to worry, that it's an honor, but she's affectionately known as the worst driver in the office by everyone, including me, and I've only been back, after being away for a year, for four days. Clearly she is saying this as much for her benefit as mine.

"Driving pool's coming up," the chief of staff says, glancing sidelong from behind his shades. "You're jumping in."

"Jumping or getting pushed," I say. It's a Freudian kind of joke, with a cold kernel of truth wrapped in the fuzzy warmth of the dumb wordplay.

"Everyone has to pull their weight. I can't let you out of it. Besides, it's becoming for a young woman to be capable."

I want to tell him that I'm capable of plenty of things, and that I think driving itself is unbecoming.

I've been reading Herman Melville during my commute on the train—one of many activities one cannot pursue while driving—reading about Melville's reluctant scrivener, and right now I want to do my best Bartleby, to repeat *I'd prefer not to* as a tireless refrain, until at last the chief of staff gives up in exasperation. But we've talked about this before. My first day back I wandered into his office, trying to act casual as I threw myself, with as much dignity as possible, at his mercy. I'm terrified of driving, I explained, and the senator would probably be terrified of driving with me. That, the chief of staff told me, was the absolute last thing I wanted to make the senator say—and it was clear then that I had no choice, or at best the choice was a Hobson's one: "Drive the senator, or lose the job you just won back."

"Sorry, babe," he says as we pull off Irving Park Road and onto a side street, looking for parking. "This is just the way it's gotta be."

As he parallel-parks, we are in the midst of environmentalists and animal-lovers all trying to do the same. All these putative friends to the Chicago River seem to have driven here too, mostly one person to a car.

I pitch the hat in the backseat and shake out my hair as the chief of staff rolls the top up and flips the power locks. He puts his hand at the small of my back, against my pink summer sweater, and we walk toward the event. Thinking about what I've gotten myself into, I want to run the other way, but I try to stay in the moment and focus on the now: *At least I am walking. I am not driving. Yet.* My boss is still talking, he is almost always talking, and he is promising to make it easier on me, to come with me for my first behind-the-wheel.

"He's a nice guy," he is saying of the senator. "You know that. But when he smells blood—if he senses somebody's uncertain—he'll attack. It's that trial lawyer background. Anyway, I'll ride along. Run interference. As for you, just act like you know what you're doing, and don't wrap it around a tree."

JULY 11, 2007:
OLDSMOBILE CUSTOM CRUISER, OXBLOOD

My mom and I are out after dinner in the long and humid midweek dusk, running suburban errands of some kind—the grocery store? Target? the library?—in her oxblood Oldsmobile Custom Cruiser station wagon. She calls it her dream car. She has called it her dream car since she got it in 1992, and though it is now fifteen years from being new, my gay best friend Clark, who lives in LA, wants it when she's done—because they no longer make station wagons, and it is so campy, so fabulous. "Here is the top," he likes to say, gesturing, "and here is your mom's car," he finishes, extending his arm as far up as it will reach. But he'll have to wait. My mom has agreed that yes, she will bequeath it to him in the end, but not until the monster is on its very last legs.

The Custom Cruiser is a total boat, and its gas mileage has been declining predictably for years, but I have many warm memories of family vacations made possible by its behemoth strength, its dependability, and its spacious interior, road trips including but not limited to Branson, Missouri; Yellowstone National Park; the South Dakota Badlands; the Grand Tetons; and the Wisconsin Dells, all arrived at courtesy of its tank-like confines. I grudgingly love its skylight (not a top window that opens, not a sunroof, but an actual skylight), its third row of backward-facing seats, and the smooth leather upholstery that sticks to your thighs in even minimal heat.

My mom has just asked me about my day. My husband and I are living, again, in my parents' basement, the second summer in a row, though Martin and I and his trusty Ford Taurus are moving into our new place in the city on the first of next month.

I am telling her about work, trying to be obliging, since she is letting us stay with her rent-free. I don't want to think about it, let alone say it out loud, but I tell her anyway about the task with which I've recently been charged. Saying it makes it feel more real.

"I'm in the driving pool, Mom. I'll get the honor of driving around the one and only senior senator from Illinois. We picked last week, and I'm scheduled for the end of August, during the recess. Should be pretty busy." I had only chosen that week because I drew the number seven—lucky, my ass: close to dead last. The conventional wisdom in the office is that, even though it's an honor, you pick a week you think will be light, though the senator's schedule is so hectic, it's a gamble regardless.

"Oh," she says, and I can tell she is thinking. She is an ardent adherent to the if-you-can't-say-anything-nice school of manners, and she is picking her next words with care. "And where will you be driving him? The suburbs or the city?"

"Both," I reply with cheer—so much cheer that it comes out fake. "Wherever he needs to go, that's where I'll take him." I have scarcely driven in the past ten years, and I have never—not once—driven in The City, Chicago or otherwise.

"Sweetie, maybe you should practice," she says.

"Mom, are you kidding me? Have you bought gas lately? I'm not doing donuts in the church parking lot when prices are this high."

"Well, I just think it's wise to be prepared. You *are* going to be responsible for the second most powerful man in the United States senate."

"Okay, fine," I say. "Can I borrow your car?"

"Well," she hesitates. "Why don't you just use the Taurus?"

"Martin needs the Taurus. And I'll mostly be driving big vehicles, minivans and things, so we can fit the press team and everybody in there. I need to practice in something large. This thing is a land yacht."

"Well," she says again.

"Okay," I say. "Never mind. I'll just wing it."

I change the subject to something related, but that I know will please her. "We have to drive American cars," I say. "We have to tell the rental place: only American."

"Oh really?" she says, perking up.

"Yeah, because of the unions. Nothing from Japan, nothing from Europe. Everything we show up in, especially with the senator, has to have been made in the U S of A."

"Well, I think that's great."

I am of the belief that, thanks to globalization, there's no such thing as an American car anymore. But those are the cars I am supposed to drive, so those are the cars I will.

JULY 14, 1930:
FORD MODEL T, BLACK (OF COURSE)

The day is bright and the day is bone-dry. Under the deep blue dustbowl of the Nebraska sky, my great-grandfather is about to be murdered by a Ford Model T. Glossy and black, a mechanical assassin, it stabs him in broad daylight before the horrified eyes of his wife and children.

He is cranking the car to start it and the car kicks back, driving the shaft of the crank into his abdomen, knifing through his trousers, nicking his stomach, and rupturing his guts. A sturdy man and tough, the son of immigrants from Bohemia, he is accustomed to hard work and physical pain, and he does not die right away.

Based on where the blow has landed, there will be some speculation that, had he been wearing a belt with a buckle instead of suspenders to hold up his pants, he might have been saved. In fact, there will be some indication that he hasn't even realized how badly he's been hurt. But the internal injuries are serious, and the doctor there in Dwight—a tiny Czech community in vast Butler County—is not equipped to deal with internal bleeding or peritonitis. He lingers a little, and eventually dies. My grandfather, my mother's father, who is not anyone's father or grandfather at this point, is nineteen.

My coworkers wonder why I despise driving. I kind of don't know, and I kind of think the answer is too complex to give them what they are looking for: an explanatory story that provides perfect insight; something emotional, not intellectual. Did I experience some brutal and sudden childhood trauma that has led to my current irrational fear of cars? No. First, it is not merely a fear; it is an intense and cultivated distrust and dislike. Next, it is not irrational; I find my skepticism and my studied avoidance to be sane, normal, and soundly reasoned. It is everyone else who is illogical, injudicious, and reckless—with their lives, the lives of those around them, and the life of this planet.

Still, when pressed, I do my best, and I recount this anecdote. The story itself is not a lie; it really is horrible and it really did happen. The lie is that it has anything directly to do with my own distaste for being behind the wheel. But while it's not exactly connected to my odd (to others) resistance, I keep telling it anyway because it's easier. It's more convenient than most alternatives. It saves time, and it gets me where I need to go—where other people want me to go. All things you could say about driving itself.

Still, sometimes, when work is slow and I need to look busy, I look them up online: these early fathers of the automobile in their colorless photographs, these titans of production, these captains of industry, all white, all old, all long-dead, with their hair slicked back, their thin lips faintly smirking. I stare at them, and I am disgusted, not so much for what Henry Ford did to my great-grandfather, but more for the dependency to which they—Karl Benz, Armand Peugeot, Ransom Olds, Rudolf Diesel, and all the rest—inadvertently consigned us. Yes. The car is an unchecked force that shapes my life whether I like it or not, and I do not like it.

SPRING SEMESTER, 1996:
DOWNERS GROVE NORTH HIGH SCHOOL BASEMENT,
DRIVING SIMULATOR, BEIGE

Mr. Liston, who wears Cosby sweaters and a thick brown beard, and whose lips become smacky and beaded with little white threads of spit when he lectures, is patient and monotone, but becomes visibly frustrated by how bad I am at the simple tasks he sets before our class.

He switches the simulators to manual so we can learn, just in case, how to drive stick. I keep failing to follow his instructions, repeatedly killing my machine, as the students around me glide effortlessly among the gears.

"You know, not everyone needs to know this," he sighs as he appears by my side. He sets my simulator back to automatic. I hit a simulated pedestrian, I hit a simulated bicyclist, and he suggests I just turn it off entirely and take a break. "We'll focus on the road experience," Mr. Liston says, spit gathering at the corners of his mouth as his lips meet to form the words.

Out in the snowy parking lots and poorly plowed side streets, Mr. Liston slams the passenger-side brake in the cream-colored Drivers' Ed station wagon many, many times during my behind-the-wheels. Even though he is usually saving me, himself, and the three students in back from disaster, he does it with the casual firmness of a businesslike handshake. But I can tell: he is losing hope in me.

I may be a terrible driver, but I am an excellent student. "How many people a year die in auto accidents?" the weekly *Rules of the Road* quiz asks. "Forty thousand annually in the United States alone," I answer. Then, for good measure, "1.3 million world-wide, and that will only increase as the rest of the globe becomes 'industrialized.'" "Correct," the graded quiz comes back, "but a little morbid?" Maybe so, but those are the facts.

The rest of the students seem to be naturals at this act which I find to be anything but: strapping yourself into a loud and stinking two-ton metal device and hurtling down roads at high speeds surrounded by other people strapped into loud and stinking two-ton metal devices, very often people who are rude and impatient and always in a hurry. Kids I had considered to be thugs, kids I'd thought of as meatheads, were truly gifted at this, while I faltered and fell behind.

I was a success at school, but I was a failure at life.

These kids watch with ghoulish interest Mr. Liston's scared-straight videos. I black out and have to go to the nurse during short vignettes depicting insouciant teens in '80s outfits drinking at parties and then driving off cliffs in the dead of night; teens with feathered hair careening around hairpin turns and spinning end over end into rivers and ditches; teens with polo shirts and blue eye-shadow failing to Stop, Look & Listen at railroad tracks, winding up smeared and bloody and definitely dead in the prime of their young lives.

Still, I am determined. I am going to know, at the age it is considered fitting and proper for an American young person to know, how to drive a car. *Any idiot can drive*, I remind myself, *and I am not an idiot.*

SPRING SEMESTER, 1998:
CHEVY CELEBRITY, SNOT-GREEN (OR "CELERY")

In our senior superlatives, the class of 1998 sees fit to list me under "Most Likely to Succeed," "Best Person to Copy Homework From," and "Most Likely to Become President." They see fit to list my ride under "Worst Car": a bulky American shitbox in a sea of Volvos, Lexuses, Volkswagens, and Mercedes.

The car comes from my parents, and was the cheapest they could find through a friend of theirs, a dealer in Nebraska. It comes from the year 1984, the year my youngest sister Megan was born. The car campaigns for itself, hard. My middle sister Beth will win "Worst Car" again three years later, followed by Megan just one year after her, at which point the rusty patches will have grown to super-continents, and the pale green fabric of the ceiling will be held up by an ugly and erratic Morse code of multicolored pushpins. The two front doors do not open from inside, so you have to crank the window down and reach for the exterior handle to release yourself, and when the front passenger side window gets stuck forever in the up position, somebody has to walk around and let you out.

I hate this car, but not because it is crappy; I would have hated any car. I tell myself I am driving it "ironically," but there's no functional difference, really, between doing something for the sake of irony and just doing it, period.

1998–2007:
THE WASHINGTON DC METRO, THE LONDON TUBE,
THE BOSTON T, METRA, THE CHICAGO EL, THE PIERCE
COUNTY WASHINGTON BUS, OTHER PEOPLE'S CARS,
MY HUSBAND'S TEAL HYUNDAI, MY OWN TWO FEET

I do not drive for almost ten years.

Angela, my high school best friend, is one of the few people who doesn't tell me I should drive more. She is an archivist. She has a fondness for facts. She informs me that the majority of Americans, when asked, will claim that they are "good" or even "excellent" drivers. Statistically speaking, this is impossible: some people must be "fair" drivers, or even "poor." The bell curve must be accepted as belling, as curving. Me, though, I'll admit I'm "average," and leave it at that.

AUGUST 3, 2007:
MARICELA'S CAR, I DON'T KNOW WHAT KIND

Our high heels clicking on the permeable pavement, Maricela—the senator's Chicago director—and I are making our way back to her car after a guided tour of the new LEED-certified green building on the campus of a small evangelical university. The school lies in Elgin, one of two major cities in Kane County, forty miles from Chicago. Kane County has just been assigned to me as my outreach area; I will be responsible for "reaching out" to them. Reaching out means driving out, in a car—for me always rented since I haven't got one of my own—to have meetings with various community leaders, local electeds, nonprofits, unions, universities, and service groups. Maricela is here this time, my first, because she is training me. We have spent the morning learning about bio-swales, coolth, and reflective concrete.

I'm taller, I walk faster, and I end up slightly ahead of Maricela as we reach the cobbled parking lot, where I stand facing row upon row of identical-looking vehicles, unable for the life of me to recall which one we arrived in.

"Kathleen, are you lost? It's this one," she says, pointing, unlocking the doors, and climbing in. I do the same. I don't pay attention to cars, their models and makes; they are not on my radar. Maricela laughs a little as I try to explain this, but behind her smile there is genuine concern. There probably should be; I'm not offended.

Calmly, competently, all while changing the radio stations, answering cell phone calls, and chatting with me, she drives us to downtown Elgin, where we meet with a newly elected Democratic state representative and his chief of staff. Afterward, we stop for lunch and get milkshakes for the road, because they are supposed to be the best in the state, because it is Friday, and because it is close to 90 degrees. The whole day has been like a field trip, or an outing among girlfriends.

"This was fun," I say. "Thanks for taking me."

"Sure thing. And just think how fun it'll be next time, when you'll be doing this on your own!"

"Yes," I say. "The lure of the open road."

Thinking about this, I cannot finish my milkshake, and it sits, sweating and melty, in the black cup holder next to Maricela's empty.

AUGUST 17, 2007:
OLDSMOBILE INTRIGUE (MY MOM'S), WHITE

In less than two weeks, I will be driving the senator. Today, I am advancing him, driving alone in a separate vehicle, racing to get to his morning events before he does. I am losing the race. Somehow, though I got a substantial head start, I manage to arrive at the telecommunications roundtable a full ten minutes after them. I pass their white Dodge in the parking lot, and I rush inside apologizing. "I'm so sorry," I say, about to explain that traffic had been a nightmare thanks to the tornadoes and rainstorms of the night before, but Maricela stares daggers at me and says, "Never mind. Just leave now, and get to the next event."

I speed all the way to the Morton Arboretum, desperate to arrive with enough time to make sure everything is set up as planned for his 10:00 A.M. press conference about the Emerald Ash Borer. Advancing is like a boring yet stressful video game. I do not wrap it around a tree, though it's not for lack of trees; they are all over the roads. But I make it on time and am there, smiling like everything's okay, to meet the senator when he arrives a half-hour later.

Back at the office, Nathan, the webmaster, asks me how it went, and I tell him. "Did the big guy let you have it?"

"No," I say. "He patted me on the back and told me to keep at it."

"Figures," says Nathan. "He never yells at girls. You guys get away with murder."

But I do not want to get away with anything, or to be pretty good at driving *for a girl*. I just want to be pretty good.

AUGUST 29, 2007:
FORD WINDSTAR, WHITE

Labor Day weekend: the senator will be flying to Iowa to campaign for Obama, so I'm responsible for driving him for only two days, but the first day runs a total of fourteen hours. I pick him up at his condo at 7:00 A.M., and I hardly leave the car until I drop him off back there at 10:00 P.M. We go to Argonne National Labs in the suburbs and we visit the *Chicago Tribune*. We stop by a charter school on the West Side, do a radio interview at WGN, and attend a fundraiser and the Cook County Dems Dinner in honor of Mayor Daley.

At that dinner, I am allowed, finally, to exit the minivan and come inside and eat. One of my tablemates, a nice man who works for People's Gas, requests my card and asks what I do for the senator.

"Whatever needs doing, but today I'm driving."

"You?" he says and looks at me incredulously. "You are responsible for the corporeal body of the second most powerful man in the U.S. Senate?"

Thank you, sir, for putting all of my fears for today into a single sentence, I want to say. Instead, I push my steamed vegetables around my plate and say, "Yup! Can you believe they trust me?" and we both laugh like it's a big joke, because I'm so obviously competent, and then I excuse myself and say I'd better get back to the minivan.

The second day I drive the senator—and Maricela, and the entire press team—to a news conference in the northern suburbs, and then take him to the airport, but not before I manage to get us lost on the way.

For forty-eight hours, I feel like an alien masquerading among earthlings, trying to act suave and in command as I fill up the gas tank (I pull to the wrong side; the machine refuses my card), pay tolls (my handful of quarters, nickels, and dimes flashes silverly and rains down the outside of the bin), and parallel-park ("Well, that's what bumpers are for," chirps Nathan).

When at last I return the minivan to Enterprise, I feel like I've recovered, finally, from some persistent and life-threatening illness. The sky never looked so blue, and my feet were never so happy to be in direct contact with the asphalt. But when I walk back into the office, the chief of staff, who'd been with me as promised during the entire first day, wraps his arm around my shoulders and pulls me aside.

"I just got off the phone with the Duke," he says.

My stomach drops. "What did he say?"

"Well, he didn't say, 'Don't put her behind the wheel with me again,' which he has been known to do. So you're on the team."

"Great," I say, and stand in a daze in the hallway.

Nathan wanders by. "Kathleen, how did you survive in the world up until this point? How on earth did you get by up until now?"

He stares at me, baffled, and waits for my answer.

"On foot," I say. And walk away.

OCTOBER 25, 2007:
THE (ACCIDENTAL) MERCEDES C230, BLACK

The guys at my Enterprise Rent-A-Car downtown have made a mistake. They know by now that when I am alone, doing outreach, I like to drive small cars, cars that were made in the U.S.A., and that come to me with full tanks. But today they have screwed up. All that's available are an enormous sport utility vehicle and an errant Mercedes. The environmentalist in me would rather die than drive an SUV—and if I were to try, I probably would, since I'm like one of the four horsemen in anything bigger than a sedan. Given the choice between death and pissing off the unions, I choose the latter.

Worse than that, I find myself enjoying it. *This*, I think to myself, *is a very smooth ride*. And then I think, *Shit. Shit shit*

shit. I am already starting to get used to this: not just to driving, but to being a Person Who Drives. Driving is changing me. Cars, I know, are the iron fist. The velvet glove is the convenience, and the way I get paid to do it.

Depending whom you ask, I live in one of the top two or three most congested regions in the country. And it feels like it. All around me, the gridlock is eroding the convenience, and the comfort of driving is slipping away, so there is no more glove, just the iron—or steel, or whatever this Mercedes is made of—fist. But the car is so quiet, and it smells so nice, and the stereo sounds great: car as perfect music-delivery device. My favorite traffic reporter, Abby Ryan—sultry, authoritative—is giving the updates, and the newscasters are saying "price-fixing" and "gouging" and "sweet, light crude."

NOVEMBER 21, 2007:
CHEVY MALIBU, CHAMPAGNE

The car I'm in today has a stupid name. It is one day before Thanksgiving, and I am picking the senator up at O'Hare. It was a risk to choose this week, since it contains the holiday, but I've won the gamble: he's got a light schedule. I get him from the airport this afternoon, and I'm done.

The chief of staff has told the senator that I'm a writer, and now the big guy likes to ask me, whenever he sees me, what I'm reading.

"Marshall McLuhan this week," I say.

"Ah, the 'medium is the message' guy."

"Yeah. I'm actually looking at *The Mechanical Bride*. It's pretty dense stuff."

"Oh yeah?" says the senator, flipping through the paper, reading a headline about a singer who's going to rehab. "What's he got to say?"

"Well," I say. "According to one commentator, he's morally outraged. He sees industrial man as a puppet controlled by forces of commerce and advertising. He thinks these forces don't just change how we behave, but actually burrow into our brains and change how we see the whole world. It makes me think of driving, and how everyone just does it and no one tries to think too hard of a better way to be."

"Hmmmm," he says, then sets the paper down, picks his BlackBerry back up, and I know I've lost him, just as I lose almost everyone else when I start talking this way. I realize not everybody is interested in my journey of self-discovery regarding the automobile. The senator is more concerned with his journey to the office, and as I run a stop sign on our way there, then squeeze through a stale yellow (it's the Chicago way!) he slams on the imaginary passenger-side break, putting me in mind of Mr. Liston.

"Sorry, sir," I tell him.

"It's okay," he says, smiling, avuncular, though his smile does not make it all the way up his face. "You're getting better. Now just be sure to concentrate."

FEBRUARY 5, 2008:
PONTIAC G6, BLACK

At the Super Bowl two nights ago, the scrappy underdog came from behind for the big upset. Some announcer said that Eli Manning, the scrappy team's quarterback, had finally overcome

his weaknesses and "turned the imaginary corner." All day yesterday, when they were not debating the possible outcomes of
today—Super-Duper Tuesday—my coworkers quibbled over
whether the "imaginary" in that assessment was necessary. (The
consensus: probably not—wasn't the metaphor obvious?)

But behind the wheel of my rented Pontiac G6—six whats?—
this Tuesday, a Tuesday when it seems the entire country might
be turning an imaginary corner (A woman for president? A black
man?), I feel as though I have finally turned one too. With the
senator beside me, and the chief of staff and the press secretary in
the backseat, I am really driving. I am reading the signs and deciding where to go, logically, by myself; I am making choices, not
clinging to MapQuest, and not thinking of other people's advice
(not Pat's New-York-City-specific "Don't look in the mirror, just
do what you've gotta do and assume everyone will get out of your
way" and not Charlie's "Just think of how powerful you are").

I drop my passengers at the Hyatt Regency on the river for
the Obama returns party, and drop the car in a parking garage
nearby. When I have to be somewhere, I instantly do not want to
be there; when I cannot be somewhere, it is the only place in the
world that I want to be. Right now, I want to be inside. So I leave
the car and make my way upstairs to the VIP ballroom to watch
the election returns. As I stand in the crowd, some Obama staffers
approach me to see if I would please go stand on the risers behind
the stage to be one of the young faces providing the backdrop
for his victory speech. I probably wouldn't have said yes even if
I could have—since I do not like to be anybody's advertisement,
not even Obama's—but tonight I say no because I have to stay
free, have to be able to make my way out and down to the car as

soon as my senator begins to speak, because after he speaks, he will want to go home.

I am the picture of responsibility and confidence. I am The Driver.

MARCH 14, 2008:
DODGE CALIBER, ORANGE

I am sitting in the front seat with the engine off, waiting in a parking lot outside a West Chicago high school. I've gotten here early and am killing time before it's seemly for me to go inside.

I have rented twenty-four cars in the last five months, all from the Enterprise Rent-A-Car downtown: six Chevy Cobalts, three Ford Focuses, three Dodge Calibers, two Pontiac GPRIs, one Chevy Malibu, two Chevy Aveos, two PT Cruisers, one Ford Fusion, one Pontiac G6, one Chevy Impala, one Ford Taurus, and one Dodge Avenger.

I see the Enterprise guys more than I see a lot of my close friends.

When I first began this job, I had bad dreams about highways, expressways, tollways, and gas stations, and white and yellow lines and delays that are due to construction ahead.

Now I'm in the car so often that I'm becoming careless. Later that day, in Hanover Park, or Streamwood, or Bloomingdale—it's hard to say since they all sprawl together and look the same—I get pulled over for doing thirty miles per hour over the speed limit and somehow escape with only a warning.

"You better watch yourself," the cop tells me, eyes hidden behind his mirrored cop shades. "We get a lotta fatals on this road."

MAY 2, 2008:
CHEVY IMPALA, GRAY

I am sitting with the windows down on Michigan Avenue in the breezy spring twilight outside the NBC Tower. The senator is inside, giving an interview, but with the radio on I can hear him in the car.

On air, he harangues the FTC about their lack of oversight into skyrocketing oil costs. "The watchdogs watch idly while gas prices rise. They are letting this happen without even a whimper," he says, in that way he has of making the familiar peculiar, resurrecting a dead figure of speech and reanimating it briefly, like a transfixing zombie.

MAY 20, 2008:
CUBICLE IN THE FEDERAL BUILDING,
GSA-ISSUED, STANDARD GRAY

I am in the driver's seat of the computer in my small, gray cubicle. This week, we citizens of Illinois have received the news that *We're number one!* for highest gas prices in the country. Nobody knows why. I have spent the day helping the press team by writing letters to the editor like:

> John R___ is right: we *can* become energy independent. Unfortunately, that is the only thing he's right about. His letter sounds as if his special interest is none other than Big Oil. What sane American consumer would ever blame the Senator or Congress for high prices? These companies are not only making more money than oil companies have ever made, they are making *more money than any business in the history of America*. The five largest

oil companies in 2007 had profits of $103 billion—$2 billion a week in profits! Instead of defending these companies who thrive on the suffering of average Americans at the pump, let's focus our efforts where they will really help: breaking our addiction to oil. We can have high-paying energy jobs right here in Illinois, but let's invest in new technologies, and make those jobs green!

MAY 22, 2008:
PT CRUISER, RED

I am wearing a sweater dress, warm and knit and fairly short, but I let my legs splay anyway since it is more comfortable for the long trek I am in for, and since nobody else is in the car to be affronted, a fact about my driving that is true probably 99 percent of the time. That's one of the things that kills me: I am spending all this gas and effort and money to get somewhere in this sleek and capacious machine all by myself, and the mass of drivers around me is doing the same.

"If your work isn't what you love, then something isn't right," David Byrne sings through the speakers on my favorite radio station, WXRT, a station I actually try to schedule my outreach around, just for the sake of catching New Releases Thursday. I *do* love my work. But something isn't right, and today that something is the fact that I am in a car driving vast distances to scout gas stations for the press secretary because the senator wants to do some events on stratospheric gas prices next week, during the May recess.

Over the next two and a half hours, I will drive close to one hundred miles in the interest of helping my boss protest how ridiculous it has become to drive such distances.

The PT in PT Cruiser stands for "Personal Transportation," but it looks to me like a personal hearse. The car is designed to look old-fashioned, maybe even steam-powered, from its bulbous and curvy streamlined exterior to the huge knobs and dials inside and on the dash, the absence of a digital display in favor of a large round clockface set above the other controls. It is simultaneously a reminder of the past and a harbinger of things to come, an eerie messenger telling me, like a sci-fi novel: "The dystopic American future is now!"

My hands on the steering wheel are at 10:00 and 2:00, as Mr. Liston instructed in Drivers' Ed, and in that they echo the hands of the fake old-timey clock. Even though it is 10:10, technically after the morning rush, there's no relief, and the tollway is packed, heading north and west toward O'Hare Airport and past it. There are no real hours of traffic anymore: it is like this *all the time*. Some asshole is tailgating me, and I want badly to honk at him, but you can't honk backward.

There is a little winged icon in the center of the steering wheel, beneath which is the horn, and I can't read what it says. Every time I try, I almost crash, for we are creeping along, moving just enough to make it untenable—or at least unwise—to try to concentrate on anything but driving. It is winged like a cherub in a rococo painting, winged like your soul leaving your body in the fatal crash. The Ford ahead has a name that is sound advice: focus, focus, focus, focus.

Everything about the car I have been assigned is saying to me, *You must drive nineteenth-century machines in the twenty-first century.*

The press secretary has told me to find a gas station that is picturesque but practical, a big brand name, close to the highway but a bit off the beaten path since, understandably, the owners will likely not welcome us, calling attention as we do to their unattractive expensiveness. We need to be able to stand nearby, but out of the way, with the signs in the background—both so we are not in violation of anyone's rights, and so we don't get run over by motorists using the filling station for more mundane purposes. I am supposed to find such a station, and write down its coordinates. Originally, I was supposed to take photographs, but I pointed out that this is frowned upon, because I might be a terrorist.

The bottleneck of the Jane Addams unclogs a bit, and I worry about ever being able to scout up the right site. The station I picture is from an Ed Ruscha painting, a stylized and lonely monolith beaming like a beacon through the empty desert night. The station I find, clearly, does not look like that. It is red and yellow, a Shell just off the expressway, where regular unleaded today is $4.09, a price that will seem low one week later when the conference takes place. There is a vacant lot across the small street next to it, green and overgrown and full of tall weeds which I can't identify and dandelions which I can. The reporters can stand there, and the senator can stand on the sidewalk, so as not to get his nice suit—the pants of which are always just a little too long—dirty or dusted with dandelion fluff.

Automobiles (*auto*, meaning *self*, and *mobilis*, *moving*) are about being alone—you control the temperature, you control the music. The place is no Ed Ruscha, but it is very lonely.

I call the press secretary on my cell phone, and she okays it, but there's nobody here or in the office I can really tell what I want to say. I've come to the end of my loudly professed distaste for driving. I've stopped volunteering how much I hate to drive, stopped explaining what a New Thing driving is for me. Because while I still hate it, it's not new, and I've begun to bore myself. Because how much distance is there, truly, between doing something you protest to hate, and just doing it? Either way, the thing gets done.

Has becoming a driver made me a better person? No, but it has made me more functional. I am more useful to the economy. I can buy more things and move my labor around more widely.

I leave the vacant lot, drive back to the city.

It has been twelve years since Mr. Liston first turned on our simulators, but at long last, I am just like everybody else. So there. Are you listening? Can you see me? Are you happy?

HOWEVER
MEASURED
OR FAR AWAY

"ALL MEN'S MISERIES," Blaise Pascal said in the seventeenth century, "derive from not being able to sit in a quiet room alone."

I wouldn't say that I am miserable, exactly, but I'm certainly no good at sitting in solitude. Partly, quiet rooms are hard to come by. But even when I'm in one—when I'm in my muffled cubicle, subdued and gray, in the senator's office way up high on the thirty-eighth floor, the building sighing all around me, the elevators humming my colleagues to the street—do I pause? Am I silent? Do I meditate? Do I pray? I do not. I am not. I do not. I do not. I check my email. I read blogs. Work on poems. Socially network.

And today, I'm on the phone with a woman in California, a customer service representative from tickets.com—her voice courteous and professionally cheerful, yet obviously strained—going over available seats in Wrigley Field for the second in the Cubs' three-game series against the Cincinnati Reds, scheduled to take place on the evening of July 9. I've been on the line for over ten minutes and she is recommending that I please make up my mind.

"Miss, you wanna let me place your order? If we don't hurry up, all the spots are gonna be gone."

She has a point. The Chicago Cubs are number one in the National League, and it's been one hundred years since they last won the World Series in 1908 and everyone, *everyone*, wants to see them this season in case this is The Year.

Eventually, I give the patient woman my credit card number, dropping over $100 on two nosebleed seats in the left-field upper-deck. I've been so indecisive that the spots I've gotten are both 101 in rows seven and eight—not even next to each other, though I figure we'll sort it out when we get there; I don't really care how much I can see the game anyway. I haven't bought these tickets be-cause I particularly want them or because I root, root, root for the Cubbies or because I give a shit about sports. I've done it because my cousin Jennifer—one year older than me, sweet and kind, ac-complished and pretty, and like the big sister I never had when the two of us were growing up—has recently broken an extended period of e-silence, concluding an email to me with the phrase:

"I am thinking of things I'd like to do for the last time!"

Seeing the Cubs play on a perfect summer night in Wrigley is one of these things.

In the same email chain, Jennifer has written, "I do want to come and say 'good-bye'!" When she talks this way, it sounds like she's dying—like she's planning to kill herself or like she's been diagnosed with some terminal disease.

Jennifer has been growing apart and away from me for years, but she is speaking like this because she has just announced that she's decided to go even further apart and away, and to go there indefinitely, not just from me, but from everyone and every earthly thing. She is twenty-nine years old. She has almost completed her PhD. And she is about to spend the rest of her life learning, among other things, how to sit alone in a quiet room. Jennifer is going to become a Roman Catholic nun.

MySpace permits users to have infinite friends. Facebook caps friend totals at a maximum of 5,000. The website of the Sisters of St. Francis of the Martyr St. George in Alton, Illinois, says my cousin Jennifer will have 120 friends to make here in the States and up to 1,500 to friend worldwide. Looking at their blog, though, later that night, it's clear that her Top Friend will have to be God.

Parts of said blog read like a chaste and wimpled social networking site, with sections containing the nuns' favorite activities, introducing each year's novices, chronicling their pursuits, and showcasing their diary-style meditations.

But I can't stop staring at their start page. Pictures of nuns, smiling and crinkly-eyed, span the top, and on the left is your standard-issue navigation bar, but the right is consumed with a gruesome and tattoo-worthy vision: the pulsating and anatomically suspect Sacred Heart of our Lord Jesus Christ, surrounded by thorns, crowned in flames, topped with a cross, pierced by a spear and bleeding mightily. This kind of imagery has always appealed to me—morbid and ghastly and full of symbols to be interpreted by the initiated; puzzling to those not yet in the know.

"O, Sacred Heart of Jesus," my mother would pray at the start of car trips and other potentially fatal endeavors. "We place our trust in Thee!" my two little sisters and I, snugly buckled in the backseat, would pipe.

Ever since Jennifer sprang the news, I've been scouring the Internet for information about her order: what they do, what they believe and why. When I wrote back to her the first time after her announcement, I drafted my reply with the goal of sounding knowledgeable: "Will you do any discernment retreats, or will you start your postulancy right away? What kind of work in apostolates outside the convent do the sisters there do?"

I used to *be* knowledgeable. I went to Mass every Sunday and all holy days of obligation, even when I was sick, for the first nineteen years of my life. But my faith, and with it my perfect attendance, began, inevitably, to fall away along with other habits of my childhood, like my fear of the dark or my encyclopedic knowledge of dinosaur species. The closest I've been to attending Mass lately is referring archaically at a party to a bottle opener as a church key.

So I did know some of this stuff, and believe in it at one time, but in writing her back I acted like I knew more. I want her to know that I know what she's choosing, and that I know what I've chosen not to choose by being unable to be a person of faith.

I learn that "postulancy" comes from the Latin "postulare," *to ask.* As in, Jennifer is asking the provincial mother's permission to enter the convent. But I feel like the postulant, the one with the questions. I wonder about the same details of life in the nunnery that everyone else seems to: Will she miss having sex? Did she ever have it in the first place? Do nuns ever masturbate and how big of a sin do they think it is if they do? I do not ask Jennifer point-blank, and I do not think I ever will, even indirectly; I am trying to show respect, trying to be tactful. But because some of my friends were evidently raised by wolves, they come right out and ask me:

"Did she ever, like, date?"

My friend Elisa wants to know if Jennifer is a virgin. At first, I purposely ignore her drift.

"Yeah, some. But always Catholic boys. She had a pretty serious relationship with this guy Patrick, who'd been in the seminary, but dropped out. She always dated guys who had some reason they could never commit to her though—like she'd self-select men who would never, like, marry her."

"Interesting," Elisa says, coming to the point. "But you think she's totally, er, chaste?"

"That I do not know for certain," I say, because I don't. "You can still be a nun if you've 'done it,' though. They forgive you. As long as you've never been married and/or had a kid. Just in case you decide you want to become a sister, it's not too late for you. Yet."

And then there's my coworker Nathan. Riding the El home from the federal building one night, nearing his stop right by Wrigley—lights on, stands packed—I tell him I'm going to a game in a couple of weeks to fulfill one of Jennifer's last requests.

"Yeah," he says. "That's really nice of you. But what if her last request was that she wanted a three-way with you and your husband?"

Others of my friends are more measured in their skepticism. Christen, herself a fellow fallen-away Catholic, is mystified, as I am, by the fact that someone so high achieving as Jennifer, on the verge of earning her doctorate in engineering, is about to do something that looks, from where we sit, perilously close to throwing it all away.

"If it was any other profession," Christen says, "I'd say, 'Kickass. See, even though we're all old and shit, we can change our lives. Take that, parents who kept the same jobs they got at twenty-two.' But then, you have to throw in the Catholic thing—what's up, conditionality?"

Like Christen, my questions about Jennifer's choice tend more toward the abstract: What was her perceived summons? How did she hear the call? But I also have questions about logistics, the physical reality of the convent downstate. Not so much about the sex she'll no longer be having, but about the possessions she will no longer be permitted to own and the personal schedule she'll no longer be permitted to make; about the poverty and the humility and the rigid structure her days are about to take. My biggest question for Jennifer, weirdly, is writ large in red on the convent website:

BORED?

Boredom is one of my biggest rational fears (zombies are my biggest irrational one), and it's as though the Sisters of St. Francis of the Martyr St. George know this: "Take a peek at our schedule of the day and see if there is time to get bored! Within even such an ordered life, the Lord is constantly full of surprises, so we never know what adventure He has in store for us."

I click the "Order of the Day" link and find that the nuns rise at 4:40 every morning and must report at 5:05 for the Morning Office. Meditation is at 5:30, Holy Mass is at 6:00, and a hurried breakfast follows at 6:45 before the sisters who work in apostolates outside of the convent leave for the day at 7:00 and those who work in the convent head off to their duties at the same time. The language of the site is old-fashioned, referring to the noon meal as "dinner" and the evening meal as "supper," like my grandparents used to. They gather to read Scripture at 5:45 P.M. and every night they eat together after the Evening Office at 6:00, have Community Time at 7:30, and Retire to Bed by 9:30 P.M. Then they repeat and repeat and repeat and repeat.

Looking for some of the promised adventures on their "Happenings" page, I find pictures of postulants fitting in and getting to know one another: "There is nothing like getting acquainted over endless piles of clothing to be numbered for the laundry," one caption explains. In all of the photographs, the new sisters—scrubbed and plain-faced without a hint of makeup—wear simple black jumpers over turtlenecks of white. Other photos show highlights of more glamorous service, beyond the laundry, at the Apostolic Nunciature in Washington DC: "Swan cream puffs—a beautiful dessert for Pope Benedict!" accompanies an image of an elderly nun handing over a silver platter of graceful pastries for presentation to the equally elderly Holy Father during one of his visits to the United States. "Though cold and snowing, Sr. M. Teresa and Sr. M. Vianney braved the elements. The brats must be done!" says the text next to an image of two bundled-up nuns, one grinning and one gazing seriously into a box of raw bratwurst, both holding metal tongs and running the grill outside in a shower of snowflakes.

My favorite photo, under the history link, is an austere black-and-white portrait of the founder of the order, the stern and German Sister M. Anselma Bopp. With her wide square face, prominent high cheekbones, and discerning light eyes, she looks a bit like Jennifer. In addition to founding the order in November 1869 and sending her spiritual daughters to "work among children, youth, the aged, the sick, the poor, and the needy of every condition," Mother M. Anselma composed a series of nineteen maxims. Some of them seem just and right. "Trials have to come for everybody in every state." Fair enough. "The surest way to heaven is to be simple, humble, and faithful in your duties." Maybe so, if you believe in such a place. "Teach the children that there is no heaven for the poor alone and for the rich alone but poor and rich are together in heaven." Right on.

Others are disturbing: "A humble Sister who performs her work in a pure intention is dearer to me than a learned Sister who is proud of herself." Jennifer has gone through life with the winning one-two punch of being extremely intelligent while also "applying herself." As a result, she has actually *made* money going to school, earning something close to a double academic full-ride to the University of Nebraska for undergrad, not to mention her all-expenses paid PhD at the University of Wisconsin in Madison, where she is now, living out the last days of her life as a single layperson. She's got a lot to be proud of, so it seems perverse if not phony to say that if she is ever accidentally pleased with herself, she becomes less worthy than one of her unlearnéd cohorts.

In a country where 90 percent of the population considers itself "religious" and where the man who is, as I write this, our commander-in-chief behaves as though whatever he does, no matter how ignorant or hurtful, is fine as long as he keeps Jesus first and foremost in his heart, this stricture is troubling.

To choose to live intentionally in a community with such values seems like madness to me. I am not as humble as I'd like to be, and I am nowhere near as humble as the sisters aspire to be. I want to be proud of myself and, maybe equally, I want others to be proud of themselves too. I want to intrigue people enough to get them to Google me, and when they do I want them to find further intriguing stuff. I do want to be noticed and I don't want to be lonely. Then again, this lack of humility, when viewed this way, is clearly a trap, so perhaps Sister Bopp is onto something.

Truth be told, this lifestyle makes a kind of unmistakable sense for Jennifer. When I tell Martin the news of her decision, he's shocked at my shock; he is unsurprised. Martin has only met her a half dozen times. Still, he says, "Well, that sounds about right. Every time I've seen her, it's felt odd that she was dressed the way she was, in street clothes. I always wonder: Where's her habit? Where's her veil?"

Funny, but I also thought I could be a nun at one time, that time being when I was six or seven. My parents were extremely religious. I really liked Jesus. And I loved going to church and Catholicism in general with its rituals and categories, its gory iconography, the poetry of the liturgy, and its storied saints, each with a martyrdom more spectacular than the last. I loved the rites and repetitions, the prayers and memorization. One of the make-believe games my little sisters and I liked to play—along with school and house—was Mass. But gradually, I read beyond the CCD workbooks and learned the history of oppression of women in the Catholic tradition, and the role of the convent as a repository for unruly, unmarriageable, or otherwise extraneous daughters. I learned that being a nun was nowhere near as powerful or interesting as being a priest, and then I realized that wanting to be powerful or interesting was probably a bad reason to go into the religious life. Before, I had loved the wardrobe of priests unconditionally: the fine craftsmanship of the brightly colored vestments, the gilt-edges of the fabrics, the brocades and trims, the robes and hats, the censers and staffs. But I came to contrast them with the habits of the nuns, plain and ugly, designed to recede into a background of inconspicuousness like the dun-colored females of most bird species.

Since then, I've developed unease not just with the church but with most authority really, and I can't stand wearing a uniform. I've been at my current job with the senator for over a year and in all that time I have yet to wear a suit, even though that first June when I was back, my supervisor and the Chicago Director Maricela—powerful, suit-clad—called me into her corner office overlooking Lake Michigan and instructed me to purchase one to have on deck for when I staffed and advanced. I did it. I spent almost $300 and several hours finding a suit that looked as unique as could be, but I've never worn it. I cannot bring myself to put it on and leave my apartment.

Jennifer, though, is excited for the habit. To wear it habitually. And I guess I can see, as she sees, that it is protective and distinctive, like the uniforms of the military, emphasizing a focus and purpose, a unity with the others in her chosen line. Her uniform will keep her warm and sometimes it will keep her from harm, and other times it may make her a target. Either way, there will be no mistaking what she is, to whom she belongs. And for this nonverbal declaration, I find I feel the same grudging and ambivalent respect for Jennifer that I have for my relatives who are in the military.

They say bad women make for more interesting stories, but my cousin Jennifer is hardly a bad woman. In my immediate family, although we called her younger siblings simply David and Kristen, we often referred to her as Cousin Jennifer, like she was already a character, steadfast and defined, a dependable entity on a journey toward a solemn and certain destiny, like Mother Jones, Sister Carrie, or Father Time.

I have taught the *Confessions* of Augustine of Hippo (a.k.a. Saint Augustine) in my memoir classes, and the appeal of his life is classic: the wastrel who saw God and stopped wasting his life. Jennifer has never once seemed to waste anything. And now it seems a waste to me that she never got to. And now, here she is on the verge of a vow of poverty, of humility, of chastity. And now here am I still in some kind of prodigal phase. I am not confident that I could not be doing better, that I am not making grave errors, that I am not, in some unwitting and selfish fashion, wasting my life. But in a strange way, this gives me hope. Like I have promise, maybe. I could have a conversion, eventually. Even a deathbed one.

Jennifer, meanwhile, has always had a personal relationship with God. She has always taken after our moms' side of the family. Our moms' mother, our Granny Marie, came from a brood in which—out of six kids—four took religious vows: her sister Lucille became a nun with the School Sisters of Notre Dame, taking the name Elizabeth, after the mother of the Virgin Mary; her brothers Henry, Fran, and Alfred all became Redemptorist priests, with Alfred going on to become a bishop in Brazil. Her brother Phil married, had kids, and died relatively young of cancer. Granny, I suspect, felt guilty that she too didn't become a nun, or at the very least that she too didn't have the luck to die younger, the better to hurry up and be with Jesus.

I can recall only one instance of Jennifer being "bad" and that might not even be a memory, precisely, since I was so little. The incident is retold with great frequency at family gatherings. It was Christmastime. We were staying at Granny's. Grandpa Boo (so-named for his propensity to hide behind furniture, then jump out and scare us, to our delight) had tucked us into the bed we were sharing. All the adults, Granny and Boo's four daughters and their spouses, were having drinks downstairs. I couldn't have been more than three-and-a-half, with Jennifer almost exactly one year older. "I'm hungry," I whined. "And I'm not even tired." "Let's go get some graham crackers, then," she answered sensibly. This sounded delicious, but I was terrified at the prospect of the adults coming up and catching us out and about stealing snacks after bedtime. But she managed to convince me, so we made our caper in our footie pajamas with a flashlight, down the hall, through the dining room, into the kitchen, and into the cabinet where the graham crackers were kept in a metal coffee can. We were sitting on the floor, surrounded by crumbs, crackers in our mouths, my back to the stairs, Jennifer facing them when she looked up, dropped her jaw, then clapped her hand to her forehead. Grandpa Boo had come back up to refill his glass. We were caught. But instead of getting mad, he called the other adults up and they laughed and took photographs, before making us brush our teeth again and go to bed for real this time.

This story is extra funny because I would grow up to kind of be the "bad" one, disobeying my parents, staying out after curfew, getting into screaming fights with my dad about religion, making my mom cry, stopping going to church, becoming pro-choice and going to work for one of the top five most liberal sena-tors in the United States. Jennifer persuading *me* to do something bad? That is a reversal of expectations; that is irony.

But I do remember that her mother, Margy, my mom's younger sister, seeming completely convinced that Jennifer was secretly a bad seed. My recollections of Jennifer showcase her pu-rity, her wholesomeness and industry. And she was fun too. She always had great ideas for us to be *doing* something; engaged in some thoughtful and productive activity: we could make holiday cards for the people in the nursing home where her Girl Scout troop volunteered. We could compose a song with lyrics about candy canes to perform at the piano on Christmas Eve—she was a gifted musician; I was loathe to practice. We could teach our younger siblings dance routines. We could run through the sprin-kler in the backyard to show Grandpa Boo how much we liked that toy, the one that creeped me out because it was shaped like a clown's head. We could catch fireflies and put them in a jar to bring to Granny. We could sit quietly, while the two of them were napping, and flip through the faux-leather photo boxes that Granny kept for each cousin in the guest bedroom.

We could look at these endlessly. On the outside of each, Granny had stenciled each grandchild's initials, in pseudo–gold leaf, the kind that came on wax paper and that you rubbed into place with a bottle cap or coin. Jennifer Ann Wagner—her ini-tials spelled JAW. Kathleen Marie Rooney—KMR spelled mine. My letters murmured, were incoherent. Hers were definite, intel-ligible. I'd been jealous that hers made a word and that mine was nonsense. I'm a jealous person; I can't stop comparing myself to other people, even when their choices are ones I am confident I do not want to imitate. That may be because I want more than one life. I want to be everywhere all the time. And looking at the photos was kind of like that; like we got to be in the present, but also in the past. Our favorite picture, of course, was the night of the purloined graham crackers. Had we ever been that small? That silly?

Yet Margy remained positive that Jennifer was a brat. She would go on and on to my mother and anyone else close at hand about how incorrigible her eldest daughter was, how you couldn't tell her anything. Margy held all of her kids close; stiflingly so. To a degree, she still does, or tries to. For a while, she had all three of her more or less adult children living in Lincoln, Nebraska, under her roof again, in their childhood bedrooms. I think she'd keep them that way for eternity if she had it within her power.

Margy required Jennifer's compliance even in her physical appearance. Granny, Margy told us, had made my mother and her sisters keep their hair short and manageable, and to remedy this injustice in her own life as a mother, Margy mandated the opposite. She forbade either of her daughters to cut their hair more than once or twice a year, an inch at a time, just to get rid of the straggly tips. My mom let Beth and Megan and I do whatever we liked as long as we were responsible for it, and since none of us had any patience, Beth and I had pageboy bobs and Megan's particularly curly, unruly locks were totally cropped.

Outwardly, I sided with Jennifer that her mother's long-hair rule was awful; solidarity and whatnot. Inwardly I was envious: Jennifer's mother required her to wear her hair like a princess. Jennifer's hair was chestnut and flowing, like a heroine's in a storybook. She would complain and complain, especially as a teenager, about how much she hated it. But no matter how Margy smothered her, Jennifer never rebelled. When she would get really angry, when Margy would malign her so much she'd retreat with me to her room and cry, I'd ask "Why don't you cut it? Why don't you cut off all your hair just to spite her if you want it shorter anyway?" I'd offer to get the scissors and assist in the deed. But she'd look at me like I'd asked her to cut off her own head.

Jennifer does not conclude her emails to me with "sincerely," though she is the epitome of sincerity, nor with "yours," though she is *my* cousin, nor with just her name; her closing of choice is an exclaimed "God bless!" which never fails to chafe. Still, in the days leading up to her final visit, we write back and forth frequently and she blesses and blesses me.

Self-denial has long been one of Jennifer's strong suits. It is difficult to persuade her to do anything fun for herself, so I throw my heart and soul into planning our day. She has so much to do before she goes, she writes me—defending her thesis, arranging her finances, giving almost all of her furniture and other property away. She seems ready to balk, to deny herself pleasure in favor of duty, but I will not let her. I'll take the day off work, I tell her, and she can drive down from Madison early, though the game doesn't start until 7:05. Okay, she says reluctantly, but what will we do? What about dinner, I ask her. Okay, she says, and agrees to Ethiopian food. Meals in the convent will all come from the healthcare facility the sisters help operate. So you'll be eating hospital food for your foreseeable future? I ask her. Yes, that's right, she says, so she supposes it's a good idea now to eat as exotically as possible.

And when she emails me five days before the visit with the subject line "quick random question" and asks, "Anywhere near your place to get a pedicure?" I know I've got her. I make an appointment at the spa up the street. But I've been so prepared to have Jennifer bail that I haven't even asked if I can take the day off.

So finally, that Tuesday, one day before her visit, I make my way to the corner office to ask Maricela if I can take off that coming Wednesday.

"Actually," says Maricela, "I need you here for part of that day."

We're doing driving pool that morning and all staff who take turns driving the senator when he's in-state must be physically present.

"But," she adds, "I'm happy to let you take a half-day."

I thank her and explain why I need it, and she becomes much more understanding:

"Kathleen, how fantastic! Your family must be so proud."

"Yes," I say, looking past her, out the floor-to-ceiling window at the lake; it's a flawless July day. "I guess we must be," though pride, I want to add, is a deadly sin, and while I am proud of her, that pride is complicated.

Commuting home that night, reborn from the darkness of the tunnels into the light of the elevated section on the El, my cell phone beeps its voicemail beep. It's Jennifer. She never thought it would happen, her recorded voice exclaims, but by the grace of God she has completed and turned in her thesis—errors corrected, margins straight. She is driving home from dropping off the last copy at her professor's office as she's calling me, and though she is relieved, she has a terrible headache. It's only 5:30, she knows, but she needs to beat this migraine, so she is going home to bed and drawing the shades. "I'll be asleep right away, I hope, so don't call tonight, but I'm getting up as usual to go to 6:15 Mass, so please give me a call anytime after that if you'd like. I can't wait to see you tomorrow! I'll be there by 2:00. God bless!"

I save the message because it embodies the contradictions that comprise my cousin: Jennifer is so practical, yet at the same time so mystical with her migraines and her early bedtimes and her oft-uttered blessings, so delicate in body yet so strong in conviction. She reminds me of Simone Weil or something—she makes me afraid for her life, sometimes, because of the intensity of her belief. She brings to mind saints in whom faith manifested like a chronic medical condition—present, inarguable, with them all their lives—and how mine somehow managed to cure itself.

As I walk home from the station, along the sun-dappled, dirty streets of my Edgewater neighborhood, I know she doesn't mean to, but she makes me feel uneasy, inadequate. I am done with my life as an active Catholic, but that Catholicism is hell to get over. I understand, I think, what it means to have a vocation, but not the kind that she has. Her faith in the Word versus my faith in words—who will win? Are we even competing? Yes, we are, at least in the eyes of our family, and by doing this, by becoming a nun, Jennifer automatically gets a million points.

Like Jennifer, I desire for my life to have meaning and purpose. I want to be good. I want to succeed. But working in progressive politics, founding an independent press, trying to write and publish a bunch of books of my own—that, to my relatives, looks like self-indulgence, smacks of vanity. They don't really "get" poetry. If anything, my trying to get people to read it is an indication that I must categorically consider myself better than others. I am almost always alienating these people who should theoretically be close to me.

Jennifer on the other hand, well, that they can understand. That they can admire.

By announcing this decision, Jennifer has achieved the perfect daughter checkmate. Her mom can't be truly pleased with this, not really, for her daughter has once and for all devised a way to get out of her control; handing herself over to her Mother Superior renders Jennifer's actual mother inferior. But this is not something that Margy could ever articulate; in this family, Jennifer's imminent nunhood is to be taken as the best and most noble news.

Some people—many people? surely it's not just me—go through life thinking they can always kill themselves—literally or metaphorically, through reinvention—if they feel too trapped. Making my way up the alley to our apartment in a small brick six-flat, listening again to Jennifer's message, I suspect she might have gone through her life thinking, "I can always become a nun." Now all Margy can do is smile, say she's happy, maybe pray a rosary. And Jennifer never ever again has to hear, "When are you coming home to Nebraska? Do you have a boyfriend? What will you do with that PhD? When are you getting married? If you want to have kids, you need to get going." She is free, binding as the convent might be. No more expectations, no more demands. She has a path, a purpose, a plan. She knows what she will do and when she is to do it and for how long and with what passionate intensity for every waking hour of every day for the rest of her life.

I press 9 again to make sure the voicemail stays saved and push through the gate into the yard behind our building. I too want to pursue something single-mindedly and say, as the home page for Jennifer's convent claims St. Francis of Assisi said:

> *This is what I want.*
> *This is what I seek.*
> *This is what I long to do*
> *With all my heart.*

I tell myself that what I am feeling can't possibly be envy. I don't want the celibacy or the poverty or the humility—I suck at all three—but I want the confidence, the surety, the faith. I think of Jennifer defending her dissertation and then walking away, turning her back on all things worldly, and I am disappointed. I am angry. And, if I am honest, I am totally fucking jealous.

There, I think as I climb the wooden stairs to our back door and slip the key into the deadbolt. I say it out loud before I walk inside, "I am jealous of Cousin Jennifer. What the fuck's up with that?" And even though I've said it, I'm still not satisfied.

When Jennifer arrives in the middle of the next day, she calls as she's parking, an easy feat since most people and their vehicles are still at work. I go down to meet her. The Wisconsin plates on her otherwise nondescript red car read CARITAS, which, along with faith and hope, is one of the three theological virtues: charity—an unlimited loving kindness toward others. *Deus caritas est*—God is love. I love this concept, and wish everyone could feel it, though

I can't help wishing too that they could do so for its own sake, without needing to bring "God" into it. I think again, for the thousandth time, how old-fashioned Jennifer's decision to join a convent seems, like becoming a knight or an alchemist or a chariot mechanic.

She gets out, and I see her and she sees me and our faces light up. Jennifer looks different: she's gotten a bit heavier and her long hair's a bit more frizzy. She's not wearing makeup, though she is sporting a Cubs T-shirt—red, white, and blue. As she lets this life go, Jennifer seems to be letting herself go, her external self at least. She hugs me and I am already less irritated than I'd let myself become.

We climb the narrow stairs to the apartment I share with Martin, who's at work, and drop her stuff off on the couch where she'll sleep tonight. I brew some coffee for me, pour some water for her, and we sit in the living room and talk and talk. I ask questions I hope don't sound stupid, and she tells me how she settled on this convent so far downstate it's practically St. Louis.

There's a match service in Racine, Wisconsin, she explains, because there are so many orders and so many women who want to join them. She was going to use them, but then through friends, her spiritual advisor in her parish, and her own research she narrowed it down to one in DC, one in the Bronx, one in Indiana, and one in Alton.

"I don't know what I was thinking about DC and New York," she says, looking at me over her glass. "I'm not a city person. And at the one in Indiana, no offense to them, the sisters seemed so *boring*. I expected to really like it there, but all they did during community time was play these incessant games of cards and dice."

"Sounds like a den of iniquity," I say.

"Ha. Anyway, the one in Alton was kind of a throwaway. But I ended up loving it—their charism of perpetual adoration to the Sacred Heart really appeals to me. And during community time, they played ultimate Frisbee, but they also made greeting cards."

"It's like visiting colleges," I say. "So, do you like, get to pick a new name?"

"All the sisters have to take a form of Mary. Mariella, which I wanted, is already taken, so I'm hoping that by the time it's my turn, Mariana's still available."

I almost don't say it, but then I can't resist, "Reminds you of high school French class, doesn't it?" Fortunately, she laughs.

At 3:00, we make our way into the uncharacteristically mild day, down my street—shady, breezy—on our way to the spa. As we stand in the lobby, perusing scented bath products, the improbably beefy, blue-eyed man whose job it is to check us in overhears us talking about Jennifer's impending haircut.

"Oh my God!" I say. "Sorry—I mean, oh my gosh. You're cutting it? How short?"

"Really short," she says. "Ten or twelve inches off. I'll donate it to charity."

"That *is* really short," says the barrel-chested man, handing us glasses of ice water with thin slices of lemon.

"I can't take it with me. They make you cut it when you get your veil."

Our respective pedicurists tell us to pick our colors from shelves mottled with bottles of polish in every conceivable shade. Jennifer pulls a modest corally-pink from the rack.

"I'm practicing being conservative," she says.

"I'm not," I say and pick a devil-red.

We sit on the cushions and the combination of looking down at the heads of the technicians bent over our toes and at Jennifer sitting next to me makes me think of Mary Magdalen bathing the feet of Jesus.

Jennifer's pedicurist looks up balefully and tells Jennifer that it's good she came in because her feet really need this. "Regular pedicures will get you straightened out," she says, and Jennifer and I dissolve into laughter. This lady has no way of knowing that this is the last pedicure of Jennifer's life.

At dinner, at the Ethiopian Diamond, Jennifer enthuses about how delicious everything is—the vegetables and grains all served communally on a huge *injera* pancake—and how much she'll miss eating ethnic food.

"When I visited, for lunch all they had was either a sandwich with egg or seafood salad. They hardly ever eat any beef."

"It's hard for me to feel bad about that one," I say.

"I know—the vegetarian thing. But for me, it's a big deal."

And I know that it is. Even more serious to me, though, is the news that she will only be permitted to communicate via letters. No phone calls, no emails, no family visits and virtually no outside contact for most of her postulancy. She will not be permitted to receive any messages from unmarried men to whom she is not related and she will only be allowed to send one letter per week.

We finish our meal and she rests her chin on her hand, satisfied. I insist on paying.

"Don't be ridiculous," I say. "You're about to be poor."

"Kathy," she says. "Thank you so much. I'm really going to miss this. I'm having the best time."

The rest of the evening, we don't talk much further about the fact that this is another last for her, for us, even though, as we take the El to Addison, sunlight hitting her from the side, I feel like she's disappearing before my very eyes, a drawing in black-and-white that is being erased.

We arrive at Wrigley Field in a crush of fans, the air smelling of fried onions and beer suds. Hiking up the cement slopes of the stadium in the slanting sunset, we pass two girls and their mothers, each carrying a miniature plastic Cubs hat full of soft-serve swirl ice cream, and it looks so inviting, we almost ask where they got it. We decide we'd better stake out our seats first, though, to make sure we can sit side by side. We arrive at the left-field upper-deck and to our delight, our seats are empty, as are a number of the ones around them—we'll be able to sit next to each other after all. We set out in search of our own tiny ballcaps filled with ice cream.

We make it back just as the national anthem is beginning. Jennifer is rapt.

In the top of the first, the most fascinating beer vendor I've ever seen appears, opening Old Styles with a vicious efficiency, church key dangling from a rubber band on his tan right wrist. According to his nametag, his last name is "Suntrick" and he is a complete beer ninja freaky-fast, and he freaks Jennifer out. After Suntrick makes his way down to the mezzanine, he is replaced by a Groucho Marx–looking Lemon Ice vendor running up and down the stairs and declaring, "God bless it," when nobody wants to buy any. Jennifer muses about purchasing one of his inferior-to-beer products just to help him feel better, but I talk her out of it.

In a little while we will be back at my apartment, and she will be asking where she can go to Mass the next morning, early, before she drives back to Madison. She'll settle on an 8:15 service at St Peter's in the Loop, one stop from my office, and though I could probably do it and still make it to work by nine, I will not go with her. She will tell me the church has a labyrinth that is, to her chagrin, not available in the summer. In a month or so, the red polish on my toenails will be chipped and half grown-out and I won't want to take it off, but I'll have to—the erasure of something I want to preserve but can't. A little after that, a package will arrive, bearing Jennifer's return address: books she's giving away that she thinks we might like. One is a 1940 Modern Library edition of *The Prince and The Discourses* by Niccolò Machiavelli. "I guess she won't be needing this where she's going," Martin will say wryly as I pull it from the wrapper.

The other will be the same red that my toenails used to be, called *The Joy of Words* published in 1960: a digest of tonic excerpts from Great Works by Great Men. This one will seem more nunly with its emphasis on duty and busyness for the sake of being busy. I will be leery of its exhortations in the chapter called "HUMILITY: He Who Humbles Himself Will Be Exalted," like these are ways to preserve the current order of things, to keep the ones on the bottom from aspiring to more: do not bother attempting to change things here on earth, for you will one day have your eternal reward. I will agree more with the mindset expressed in a book by John Ruskin: "People are always expecting to get peace in heaven: but you know whatever peace they get there will be ready-made. Whatever making of peace they can be blest for, must be on the earth here." And I will regret again the decision Jennifer is making.

But then I'll turn some more pages, and there will be Henry David Thoreau: "If a man does not keep pace with his companions, perhaps it is because he hears a different drummer. Let him step to the music which he hears, however measured or far away." Well, okay. Jennifer is not going to be that free. But how free am I with my eight hours a day in cube city, working for something I think I believe in? How different can Jennifer and I be said to be?

But none of this has happened yet. At the ballpark, the Girl Scouts behind us are calling out group cheers, and the skinny twentysomething guys in "Fukudome is my homie" T-shirts down and to our left are joining in. The middle-aged professionals to our right are swaying, belching, ordering double-fistfuls of Bud Lights before alcohol sales cease. A homerun by the Reds careens into the bleachers, then gets spit back from the stands like a piece of Heimliched food. During the seventh inning stretch, NASCAR driver Juan Pablo Montoya butchers "Take Me Out to the Ballgame" and Jennifer laughs: "This is even worse than when Ozzy Osbourne did it." The LED flashes the Sharpie-sponsored

Guess Tonight's Attendance game. I correctly pick (b) 41,605, thinking that's probably bigger than Alton, which, when I check later, is reported to have had 34,511 residents, nuns included, at the 2000 census.

Just before fall comes, just days before Jennifer actually goes there, I will get to see her one more time unexpectedly. Our Granny will die, two months shy of her ninetieth birthday. Her brother Henry, one of the priests, will say at her wake, "Her life is not ended, but changed," and I will try to believe him. After her funeral, the thought of sitting in a sterile hotel room while my mom and her sisters—jealously, with care—divvy up Granny's jewelry will be too much to bear. I will decide to go roller-skating.

In Lincoln, Nebraska (home to the National Museum of Roller Skating), my sisters, my cousins, and I will go to Skate Zone, locally owned and operated since 1950. Jennifer and Kristen are shaky but game in their rented shoe-skates. My sisters and I used to skate all the time when we were younger, and we're still okay. Soon we're gaining velocity, whirling in intermittent lights and monster hits from the '80s, and it looks like the end of a feel-good movie. But the movie does not feel good, entirely.

The repetition and concentration remind me of a medieval labyrinth, a prayerful activity. Axl Rose is asking, loud and yowly, "Where do we go now?" over the blaring sound system, and I throw the mustached middle-aged guy in the DJ booth with the jean shorts and the mullet some devil horns and he shoots me some back. Some girl in tight jeans is skating backwards, and a guy in a dirty white sleeveless T-shirt is owning the center of the rink, making figure eights—little infinity signs—with his eyes closed and air guitar-ing perfectly to the intricate solo. Everyone around me knows what to do. Everyone around me is exactly in time.

In the last email that she sends me, Jennifer will sign off with the phrase "Until God wills that we meet again." I will read this, and picture her where I saw her last, at the roller-rink, her newly short hair riffling in the breeze created by her motion around the buckled wooden circle. Jennifer is choosing to proceed with grace and surrender. I set my feet one after the other and proceed with determination. I have no idea how else to proceed.

acknowledgments

$\mathcal{G}$ RATEFUL ACKNOWLEDGMENT IS made to the editors of the publications in which the following essays first appeared, sometimes in slightly different form:

Another Chicago Magazine: "For You, For You I Am Trilling These Songs"

Gettysburg Review: "Staircase"

Gulf Coast: "I Will Catch You"

Ninth Letter: "Natural Is Not In It"

Notre Dame Review: "To Build a Quiet City in My Mind"

Quarterly West: "Did You Ask For the Happy Ending?"

Southern Humanities Review: "Always Crashing in the Same Car" and "Fast Anchor'd, Eternal, O Love!"

Thanks are due also to: Olivia Cerrone, Christen Enos, Jeffrey Esser, Elisa Gabbert, Chrissie Graham, Brendan Hogan, Andrea Mason, ElizaBeth Mary Peters, Jason Skipper, Theo Skogsberg, Chris Tonelli, Jeremy Wang-Iverson, Samuel Wharton, and my agent, Kari Stuart. And to my family, students, interns, and coworkers.

notes

PAGE   NATURAL'S NOT IN IT

7–8   The Ruskin story is adapted from Arthur C. Danto, *The Madonna of
         the Future: Essays in a Plurastic Art World* (Berkeley: University of
         California Press, 2001), 30–31.

18   Mireya Navarro, "The Most Private of Makeovers," *The New York
         Times,* November 28, 2004, http://www.nytimes.com/2004/11/28/
         fashion/28PLAS.html?ex=1259557200&en=72fa5c6ea7f6657b&ei=
         5088&partner=rssnyt.

         FOR YOU, FOR YOU I AM TRILLING THESE SONGS

23   "still all in the making," and "a promise, a possible something,"
         and "an idea, a forecast, a prophecy . . .": Walt Whitman to biogra-
         pher Horace Traubel in Ed Folsom, "'What a Filthy Presidentiad!':
         Clinton's Whitman, Bush's Whitman, and Whitman's America,"
         Virginia Quarterly Review, Spring 2005, http://www.vqronline.org/
         articles/2005/spring/folsom-what-filthy/.

23   "people are imprisoned," and "The words *democracy,*" and "swin-
         dles and perversions" abound. Where "political speech . . .": George
         Orwell, "Politics and the English Language," http://www.mthol
         oke.edu/acad/intrel/orwell46.htm. First published in *Horizon,* GB,
         London, April 1946.

26   "O Democracy, to serve you ma femme!": Walt Whitman, "For You,
         O Democracy" in *Leaves of Grass* (Hanover: Barnes & Noble, Inc.,
         1993), 99.

29   "To a Western Boy": Walt Whitman, *Leaves of Grass,* 112.

30   "Modern English, especially written English . . ." and "(i) Never use a metaphor . . .": George Orwell, "Politics and the English Language."

30   "the greatest thing by far . . .": Aristotle, *The Poetics*, adapted from the translation by S.H. Butcher, http://www.leeds.ac.uk/classics/resources/poetics/poettran.htm.

31   "I have not here been considering the literary . . ." George Orwell, "Politics and the English Language."

31   "Frames are mental structures . . .": George Lakoff, *Don't Think of An Elephant*: *Know Your Values and Frame the Debate* (New York: Chelsea Green, 2004), xv.

33   "62,144 and 68,141 civilians . . .": http://www.iraqbodycount.org/

33   "the main purpose of these States is to found . . .": Walt Whitman, "To the East and To the West" in *Leaves of Grass*.

37   "I will plant companionship thick as trees . . .": Walt Whitman, "For You, O Democracy" in *Leaves of Grass*.

42   "the party of young fellows, robust, friendly . . .": Walt Whitman, "I Hear America Singing" in *Leaves of Grass*.

FAST ANCHOR'D, ETERNAL, O LOVE!

51   "disappointment is the flip side of a strong . . ." Phillip Lopate, "Against *Joie de Vivre*" in *The Art of the Personal Essay* (New York: Anchor Books, 1995), 726–727.

56   "Herein a great enigma . . .": Roland Barthes, *A Lover's Discourse: Fragments*, trans. Richard Howard (London: Penguin Books, 1990), 20.

I WILL CATCH YOU

73   "There is poetry, which . . .": Plato in Albert Hofstadter and Richard Kuhns, eds, *Philosophies of Art and Beauty: Selected Readings in Aesthetics from Plato to Heidegger* (New York: Modern Library, 1964), 71.

74   "And the same holds true of love . . .": Ibid, 71.

86   "Is this good writing?": Stuart J. Fuller, "The Fairest Paper of Them All" (paper for Kathleen Rooney's "On Beauty Class," Fall 2006).

TO BUILD A QUIET CITY IN MY MIND

99   "Your absence breeds . . .": Weldon Kees, "Return of the Ghost" in *The Collected Poems of Weldon Kees*, ed. Donald Justice (Lincoln: University of Nebraska Press, 1975), 161.

101   "the room is cold, the words . . .": Weldon Kees, "Early Winter," Ibid, 27.

102–103   "Seattle weather . . .": Weldon Kees, "Homage to Arthur Waley," Ibid, 41.

103   Kalil Gibran, Jr. anecdote from James Reidel, *Vanished Act: The Life and Art of Weldon Kees* (Lincoln: University of Nebraska Press, 2003), 199.

103   "The room was monstrous . . .": Weldon Kees, "First Anniversary" in *Collected Poems*, 169.

103   "Love is a sickroom . . .": Weldon Kees, "Girl at Midnight," Ibid, 73.

103   "The ragged trees in lightning . . .": Weldon Kees, "The Heat in the Room," Ibid, 79.

103–104   "The crack is moving down . . .": Weldon Kees, "Five Villanelles: I," Ibid, 65.

104   "Held in the rouged and marketable . . ." and "Sleep. But there is no sleep . . .": Weldon Kees, "The Hourglass," Ibid, 94.

105   "decayingly elegant cul de sac . . ." and "There was an alcove . . .": *Vanished Act*, 132.

106   "This is the castle then, my dear . . .": Weldon Kees, "The View of the Castle" in *Collected Poems*, 39.

107   "dwarfed, immutable, and bare . . .": Weldon Kees, "First Anniversary," Ibid, 169.

107   "this rank wind / Blows . . .": Weldon Kees, "Poem Instead of a Letter," Ibid, 70.

108   "the bad dream . . .": *Vanished Act*, 84.

108   "We have a remarkably cool apartment . . .": Ibid, 124.

109   "The past goes down and disappears . . .": Weldon Kees, "The Speakers" in *Collected Poems*, 6.

109–110   "In June, the Keeses moved . . ." and "wonderful quiet," and "topheavy . . .": *Vanished Act*, 149.

110   "If the whole of poetry can be read . . .": Donald Justice, introduction to *Collected Poems*, viii.

110   "These bilious things . . .": Weldon Kees, "Corsage" in *Collected Poems*, 7.

111   "You should have seen . . .": *Vanished Act*, 211.

111   "suddenly canned . . .": Ibid, 127.

111   "The men who were haters . . .": Weldon Kees, "June 1940" in *Collected Poems*, 17.

111   "is one of the bitterest poets . . .": Donald Justice, introduction to *Collected Poems*, ix.

111   "'commodious and quieter' place . . ." *Vanished Act*, 128.

112   "a man with a slight build . . ." and "defects above the neck . . .": Ibid, 129.

112   "This is your familiar room . . .": Weldon Kees, "Midnight" in *Collected Poems*, 34.

113   "one of the last great . . .": Robert E. Kroll, *Weldon Kees and the Midcentury Generation: Letters, 1935–1955* (Lincoln: University of Nebraska Press, 1986), 125.

114   "Morning: blue . . .": Weldon Kees, "January" in *Collected Poems*, 150.

115   On how Nemerov helped Kees find an apartment: *Vanished Act*, 146.

115   "noisebox . . .": Ibid, 146.

115   "Like spines of air . . .": Weldon Kees, "The Patient is Rallying" in *Collected Poems*, 56.

115–116   "The mirror from Mexico . . .": Weldon Kees, "Robinson," Ibid, 59.

116   "The ruined structures . . .": Weldon Kees, "To Build a Quiet City in His Mind," Ibid, 161.

117–118   "This time they looked in Brooklyn Heights . . .": *Vanished Act*, 149.

118   "was on a floor high enough . . .": Ibid, 150.

119   "For a while / Let it be enough . . .": Weldon Kees, "Late Evening
        Song" in *Collected Poems*, 176.

119   "in the 'lox and . . .": *Vanished Act*, 211.

119   "a barn with practically . . .": *Vanished Act*, 211.

120   "Nailed up in a box . . ." and "These rooms of ours . . .": Weldon
        Kees, "Xantha Street" in *Collected Poems*, 76.

120   "I have come back . . .": Weldon Kees, "Back," Ibid, 120.

        FIRST PERSON IMPOSSIBLE

163   "I had a most marvelous . . .": John Berryman, "Dream Song 26" in
        The Dream Songs (New York: Farrar, Straus, & Giroux, 1969), 28.

166   "As a kid I believed in democracy . . .": John Berryman, "Dream
        Song 105," Ibid, 122.

166   "By most accounts . . .": Steve Healy, "The Dreamer Wakes: John
        Berryman," *City Pages* (Minneapolis, MN), September 9, 1998.

167   "The horizon is all cloud . . .": John Berryman, "Dream Song 370"
        in *Dream Songs*, 391.

169   "Phil Levine punched Berryman . . .": anecdote adapted from Ed
        Dinger, ed. *Seems Like Old Times: Iowa Writers Workshop Golden
        Jubilee* (Iowa City: University of Iowa Press, 1986) and http://
        en.wikipedia.org/wiki/John_Berryman.

170   "The war is real . . .": John Berryman, "Dream Song 61" in *Dream
        Songs*, 68.

170–171 "I can't go into the meaning of the dream . . .": John Berryman,
        "Dream Song 101," Ibid, 118.

173   "These lovely motions of the air, the breeze . . .": John Berryman,
        "Dream Song 146" in *Dream Songs*, 165.

174   "Them lady poets must not marry . . .": John Berryman, "Dream
        Song 187," Ibid, 206.

175   "What ever happened to . . .": John Berryman, "Dream Song 84: Op.
        posth. no. 7," Ibid, 99.

176   "My air is flung with souls which will not stop . . .": John Berryman,
        "Dream Song 127," Ibid, 144.

177   "Heaven is here / now, in Minneapolis . . .": John Berryman,
       "Dream Song 119," Ibid, 136.

178   "So now his thought's gone . . .": John Berryman, "Dream Song
       373," Ibid, 395.

180   "That is our 'pointed task . . .": John Berryman, "Dream Song 36,"
       Ibid, 40.

about the author

*K*ATHLEEN ROONEY IS the author of *Live Nude Girl: My Life as an Object* and *Reading with Oprah: the Book Club That Changed America*. She is a founding editor of Rose Metal Press, and her first poetry collection, *Oneiromance (an epithalamion)* won the 2007 Gatewood Prize from the feminist publisher Switchback Books. Currently, she works as a U.S. senate aide, and lives in Chicago with her husband, the writer Martin Seay.

© BETH ROONEY